# SPECIAL OPS

## JOURNAL OF THE ELITE FORCES & SWAT UNITS
### VOL.24

**CONCORD** PUBLICATIONS COMPANY

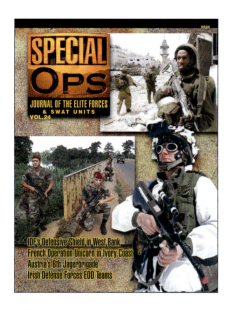

Editor: Samuel M. Katz
Associate Editor: James R. Hill
Copyright © 2003
by CONCORD PUBLICATIONS CO.
603-609 Castle Peak Road
Kong Nam Industrial Building
10/F, B1, Tsuen Wan
New Territories, Hong Kong
www.concord-publications.com

All rights reserved. No part of this publication may be reproduced, stored in a retrieval system or transmitted in any form or by any means, electronic, mechanical, photocopying or otherwise, without the prior written permission of Concord Publications Co.

We welcome authors who can help expand our range of books. If you would like to submit material, please feel free to contact us.

We are always on the look-out for new, unpublished photos for this series. If you have photos or slides or information you feel may be useful to future volumes, please send them to us for possible future publication. Full photo credits will be given upon publication.

ISBN 962-361-064-5
printed in Hong Kong

## P 3 — FROM DEFENSIVE SHIELD TO THE WAR AGAINST IRAQ
Samuel M. Katz

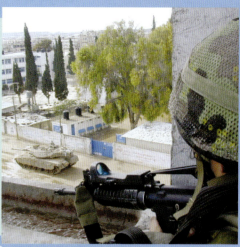

## P 29 — Operation "Unicorn"
French Forces in the Ivory Coast Civil War
Yves Debay

## P 42 — 6 Jägerbrigade Austria's Gebirgsjäger
Carl Schulze

## P 58 — The Devils of Bandit Country
Irish Defense Forces EOD Teams and the 27th Infantry Mobile Security Group
Samuel M. Katz

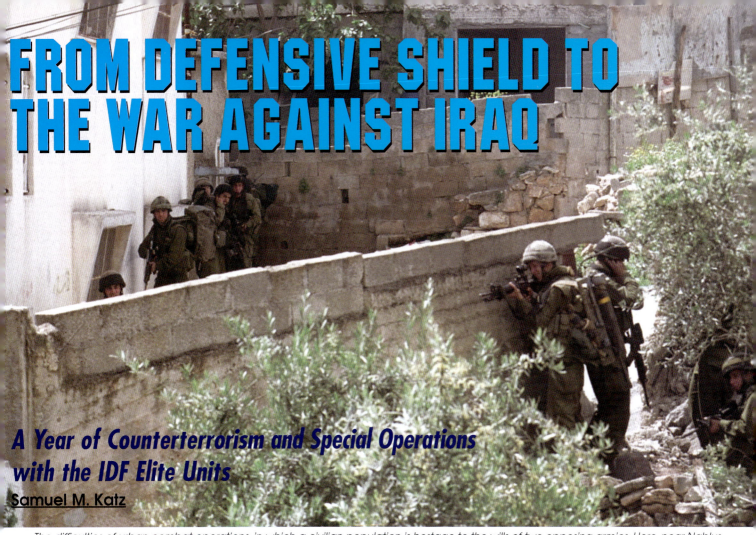

# FROM DEFENSIVE SHIELD TO THE WAR AGAINST IRAQ

## A Year of Counterterrorism and Special Operations with the IDF Elite Units

Samuel M. Katz

*The difficulties of urban combat operations, in which a civilian population is hostage to the wills of two opposing armies. Here, near Nablus, paratroopers pursue Hamas and Islamic Jihad terrorists through the streets leading to the infamous Kasbah. (IDF Spokesman)*

Rushing through the gauntlet of alleyways, looking up and around for potential threats, the young paratrooper clutched his Negev 5.56mm light machine gun closely following the other members of his squad. His brown jump boots skidded on the wet, mud-stained floor; his narrow frame burdened by the weight of his gear and Kevlar body armor. The young squad gunner was careful to keep his place in the line of soldiers negotiating the terrain with weapons at the ready. The young soldiers were expected trouble, but no one knew exactly where it would come from or when? When the grenade exploded at their feet, they reacted just as they had been taught in basic training—they followed their lieutenant and they decimated any target they saw.

*Paratroopers walk along the snow-covered pavement near the Beit Jalla Junction—a hotspot for Palestinian ambushes and PA Police sniper fire. (Reni Mor/IDF Spokesman)*

*IDF paratroopers, wearing a variety of specialized winter gear (note Hermonit one-piece coveralls), patrol the no-man's land separating Jerusalem's southernmost neighborhoods of Gilo from snipers and infiltrators coming in from Bethlehem. (Reni Mor/IDF Spokesman)*

On January 25, 2002, twenty-five people were wounded when a Palestinian suicide bomber detonated explosives outside a cafe on a pedestrian mall near Tel Aviv's old central bus station at 11:15 AM on Friday. (IDF Spokesman)

The squad gunner nervously ran forward with his comrades, looking through the smoke and haze for a target and attempting to hear verbal commands amid the ear-splitting crackling of incessant gunfire. As the gunner moved up, across an alley, a hand tugged him from behind and directed him to a doorway where the lieutenant was poised to toss a fragmentation grenade into a one-room shack. The Negev gunner knew that once the pin was pulled and the grenade tossed, there would be a four-second delay before the explosion, the burst of heat, the spraying of deadly shrapnel, and then the lung burning smoke. The gunner would have four seconds to ready his Negev Commando, and follow the lead of the red-dot

Paratroopers from the "Patan Battalion" train in quick deployment from a IAF UH-60 chopper at the foothills of Mt. Hermon on the Golan Heights. (IDF Spokesman)

A functioning Kassem-2 rocket seized by a force from Sayeret Tzanhanim in the Balata refugee camp near Nablus. (Boaz Masika/IDF Spokesman)

of the ITL AIM-1/D IR laser pointer mounted on the weapon's special rail designed specifically for house-to-house combat. The grenade's explosion was louder than the gunner expected and the force of energy and the resulting heat pushed him up against the wall, though he immediately recovered. Entering the smoke filled room, he unleashed a seventy-five round burst of 5.56mm fire from his Negev Commando, churning up the concrete block walls by the force of the fire. At the end of the fusillade, the gunner folded his Negev's stock with a sharp snap to his forearm and surveyed the damage he was responsible for inflicting.

"This isn't an art gallery," the voice said from behind in a looming, annoyed voice, "you are not here to admire your work. You are here to prepare for war and I am here to make sure you don't get killed in the process, or kill those of your force. Now remember your training, be selective in these tight spaces on how you spend your ammunition. Urban combat is the most dangerous part of war and soon you'll be fighting it for real!"

The Negev light machine gunner, being chewed out by his tactical instructor, was one of the thousands of IDF special operations unit commandos, paratroopers, infantrymen, and combat engineers to undergo intensive close-quarter urban warfare exercises at a muddied training center in the northern part of Israel in January 2002. The training, designed to adequately prepare the IDF's elite for the hell of assaulting a city, became a crash course to get Israel's front line operators ready for what was an absolute inevitability—a full-scale conflagration against Yasir

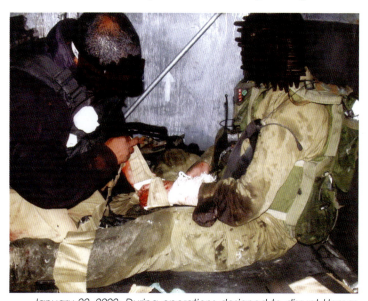

January 22, 2002: During operations designed to disrupt Hamas cells from producing explosives, IDF special forces raided bomb factories in a series of neighborhoods on the outskirts of Nablus. In the resulting firefights, four terrorists were killed. Four IDF operators were wounded, including the one featured here hit by machinegun fire. Faces have been obscured by IDF military censors. (IDF Spokesman)

*Hamas Kassam-2 rockets seized near Ramallah by paratroop reconnaissance units. (IDF Spokesman)*

*Paratroopers raid the offices of the Palestinian Authority's Preventative Security Apparatus, Force 17, Military Intelligence, Police and political agencies in the Abu Dis neighborhood of East Jerusalem. The Palestinian security services, conducting clandestine intelligence-gathering missions against the Israeli capital, as well as proactive support of terrorist operations, was functioning against peace accords signed by the Israelis and Palestinian Authority. (Nadav Ganot/IDF Spokesman)*

Arafat's Palestinian Authority and the underground armies of Hamas, the Palestinian Islamic Jihad, Fatah Tanzim, the PFLP, and the al-Aqsa Martyrs Brigade. For sixteen months the State of Israel found itself engulfed in an unconventional war for its very survival, battling terrorist attacks on a daily basis in which nearly 500 Israelis—mostly civilians—were killed. Arafat's 50,000 men under arms, part of an extensive security force funded by the United States and trained by the CIA, were now front-line combatants in a guerrilla conflict where civilians were routinely caught in the unforgiving crossfire. The Islamic fundamentalist terrorist groups like Hamas and the Jihad, funded by Iran and buoyed by a military alliance with Arafat, were able to operate out in the open and with devastating effect. They planned, prepared, and executed dozens of high-profile suicide bombings. The attacks were indiscriminate and targeted men, women and children traveling in buses, sitting inside cafés, or just standing at a corner minding their own business.

The violence, known as the al-Aqsa Intifadah, commenced on September 28, 2000, following a visit by then opposition-leader, Ariel Sharon, to the Temple Mount in Jerusalem, to profess Israeli sovereignty over a small hill holy to both Jews and Muslims. Sharon's act of arrogant politicking was the spark—the fuel to fan the flames of hatred had been spilled two months earlier at Camp David, Maryland. In a last ditch effort to finalize a peace deal between the Palestinians and Israelis before the process deteriorated into violence, Israeli Prime Minister Ehud Barak, at a summit hosted by U.S. President Bill Clinton, presented Palestinian Authority leader with an unprecedented offer to end the years of conflict.

Barak, Israel's most decorated soldier, a former commando, and chief of staff, offered the Palestinian leader ninety-seven-percent of the West Bank and all of Gaza in which to establish a Palestinian state, including parts of East Jerusalem; the concessions, more than had ever been offered, broke domestic political taboos in Israel by offering parts of the Israeli capital to the Palestinians. Arafat, presented with the deal of a lifetime, balked. History may never know why Arafat turned down so lucrative an offer, but the end of diplomacy could only mean conflict. According to western intelligence reports, Arafat forged an alliance with the Islamic Republic of Iran and consolidated a united front against Israel with both Hamas and the PIJ. When Likud-party leader Ariel Sharon traveled to the Temple Mount on September 28 the Palestinians were already poised for full-scale fighting. They just waited for a spark that could be blamed on Israel.

At first the fighting was traditional guerrilla warfare—acts of brutality marked by hit-and-run attacks; in areas where Israeli and Palestinian lines were separated by nothing more than a path, a fence or a vineyard, sniping and indiscriminate artillery fire was directed against Jewish neighborhoods. The situation in Gilo, a suburb of Jerusalem adjacent to the Palestinian village of Beit Jalla, near Bethlehem, was hit particularly hard by Palestinian rifle and mortar fire. Israeli motorists, traveling to and from their homes in Jerusalem and the West Bank, came under intense sniper fire. The IDF response to each incident was harsh.

The guerrilla-style warfare that Arafat had ordered was yielding few dividends, though. Israeli security forces, stretched thin, had not

*During a proactive roadblock by paratroopers near Ramallah, an official Palestinian Authority vehicle was discovered on a back road attempting to enter Israel rigged with explosives. (IDF Spokesman)*

*Taking aim with his scope-fitted CAR15 designated marksman system, a paratrooper prepares to engage terrorists seeking to infiltrate a settlement near Nablus. (IDF Spokesman)*

relinquished their initiative or overwhelming firepower. The people of Israel, determined not to let terror dictate their country's future, voted Prime Minister Ehud Barak out of office and replaced him with the hard-line former general Ariel Sharon. Arafat and Sharon, old enemies who battled one another in Lebanon and Beirut twenty years earlier, were once again locked in conflict. Only the guerrilla war was one that the Palestinians could not win. They soon turned to the most incessant and bloody suicide bombing campaign in history.

From November 2001 to January 2002, Palestinian terrorists executed over fifty suicide bombing attacks against Israeli civilian targets. Some of the attacks were devastating in the death toll and in choice of target—in June 2001 a Hamas terrorist blew himself up inside the entrance to a Tel Aviv beachfront disco, killing over twenty teenagers. Two months later, in August, a Hamas suicide bomber blew himself up inside a Sbarro pizzeria in downtown Jerusalem, killing fifteen and wounding nearly a hundred; many of the dead were women and small children.

Many in Israel hoped that al-Qaeda's terrorist attacks of September 11, 2001, against New York City and Washington D.C. would be a turning point in the Palestinian pursuit of their terrorism offensive—global lines of tolerance of men who sent suicidal terrorists to kill civilians suddenly changed that fateful autumn morning. Although Arafat donated blood in a public relations ploy to help those hurt by the September 11 attacks, the attacks against civilians continued.

Since 1993, the mood inside the Israel Defense Forces General Staff was that any final accords between the Israelis and Palestinians *had* to be a political solution—not a military one. But that line of thinking, one that followed Israel's withdrawal from most of the West Bank, hinged on Palestinian security forces fighting terror—not directing it. By the fall of 2001, however, the prevailing mood inside the hallways of the *Kirya*, the IDF General Staff HQ complex in Tel Aviv, was that some sort of large-scale conventional military operation would be required to disrupt the Palestinians' ability to mount terrorist attacks against Israeli targets in the

*Faced with a deteriorating situation with Yasir Arafat inside the West Bank and Gaza and increasing military tensions along the northern border with Iranian-sponsored and Syrian-supported guerrillas from Hezbollah, the IDF prepared for war. Here, atop the Golan Heights, Merkava Mk III tanks from the 188th Brigade's "Ga'ash" Battalion, deploy in column formation. (IDF Spokesman)*

West Bank, and against Israel's cities and civilian population. There were no illusions about reoccupying the West Bank and Gaza—veteran Israeli officers who had served in the territories were happy to be rid of the headache. But an Israeli military presence to dismantle the Palestinian Authority's security apparatus, one that had openly embraced terrorist operations, was required; that same presence, would also aggressively and innovatively mount operations against Hamas and the other fundamentalist groups that dispatched suicide bombers against Israel's population centers. Although Arafat himself would not be a physical target of any IDF action, the consensus concurred, his posture would have to be physically dismantled so that it could be corrected and rehabilitated. Evidence of Arafat's complicity in the violence (even though public statements to the contrary were continuously fielded by his spokesmen and lieutenants) was seized on the open waters of the Red Sea in January 2002 when, in a daring operation dubbed "Noah's Ark," operators from the IDF/Navy's elite Flotilla 13 stormed on board the *Karine A*, a freighter, ferrying nearly fifty-tons of Iranian-supplied weaponry, explosives, missiles and ammunition that was destined for the Gaza Strip.

Throughout the early months of 2002, the Israelis displayed restraint in the wake of successive suicide bombings in Tel Aviv, Jerusalem, and the country's northern areas; often deferring from executing large-scale retaliatory strikes under intense political pressure from the United States. But, like Arafat's decision in September 2000 to turn the political process into a military struggle, Israeli Prime Minister Sharon realized that there would be a Palestinian terrorist attack so barbaric and unacceptable, even to a population already numbed by the threat and fear that Israel would have to act. That attack came on the night of March 27, 2002, as families throughout Israel were gathering to celebrate the Passover holiday, commemorating the Jews' escape from enslavement at the hands of the Egyptians.

On March 27, 2002, a West Bank native who had worked in the Israeli coastal town of Netanya before the Intifadah began, walked into the lobby of the Park Hotel, a small seaside resort carrying a large bag; he was dressed as an observant Jew. The Park Hotel was packed with Israeli families who had decided to spend their holiday feast at a hotel, dining on the traditional Seder meal in the ornately decorated hotel banquet hall. The Palestinian walked calmly to the dining area, never flinching. Positioning himself among the holiday guests, wearing their finest clothes, he flipped a toggle switch and detonated over fifty-pounds of high-grade nail-studded TATP packed in his satchel. The fireball, followed by the unrelenting energy and heat, resulted in a smoky cauldron of death and destruction. Most of the ground floor was blown to shards of glass and lumber; holiday

*Paratroopers return to their chopper following a search mission for possible Hezbollah infiltrators on the foothills of Mt. Hermon. (IDF Spokesman)*

*The Lebanese winters are harsh and cold—especially in the hills of the south, near Mt. Hermon and Syrian territory—where the peaks resemble the alps. To be able to function in such conditions, the IDF Alpinistim unit trains in covert and special counterinsurgency operations in the whitest of winter conditions. (IDF Spokesman)*

*During winter warfare training near Mt. Hermon, an Alpinistim unit operator takes aim with his M16 assault rifle as he covers the withdrawal of fellow team members recovering a wounded comrade in a combat simulation. (Nadav Granot/IDF Spokesman)*

tables draped in delicacies, were thrown throughout the hotel. Bodies were torn to shreds by the blast. By the time police and rescue personnel reached the scene, the floor of the dining hall was ankle-deep in blood. The atrocity, dubbed the Passover Massacre, was the very act that the Israeli government of Prime Minister Sharon knew would require a point-of-no-return response. Days later, the IDF moved into the West Bank. The campaign, Israel's largest in twenty years, was known as "*Mivtza Homat Magen*"—Operation Defensive Shield!

From the onset it was clear that any large-scale IDF retaliatory strike would be a special operations unit and infantry campaign, supported by heavy armor. The Palestinian security services and Hamas could not be fought using F-16s.

The IDF's special operations and counterterrorist units had, of course, been operating inside Palestinian territory for nearly ten years—regardless of the peace process and the onset of the Intifadah. Among these specialized units, the most active was *Duvdevan*, or Cherry, the IDF's undercover unit responsible for the West Bank; *Shimshon*, or Samson, was the IDF unit deployed in Gaza until Israel's pullout in 1994. Unlike certain units inside Israel's military and civilian undercover section, designed to remain undercover behind enemy lines for lengthy operational assignments, *Duvdevan*'s mission involved direct action operations, raids,

*In southern Israel, units stationed near the Gaza Strip also prepared for war as the situation deteriorated between Israel and the Palestinian Authority; in Gaza, home to Hamas and the Palestinian Islamic Jihad, any invasion promised to be met with fierce and fanatical opposition. Here, on a live-fire range, a unit from the Giva'ati Brigade's antitank reconnaissance platoon launches a TOW ATGW. (Nadav Ganot/IDF Spokesman)*

*Prior to the violent outbursts of February and March, IDF units trained for large-scale operations. Here, IDF Chief of Staff Lieutenant-General Shaul Mofaz (left) and Ground Forces Commander Major-General Yiftach Rontal, observe a combined armor-infantry live fire exercise. (Nadav Granot/IDF Spokesman)*

Fearing possible Iraqi chemical first strikes and even the possibilities of Palestinian terrorist groups deploying weapons of mass destruction, the IDF fielded a large-scale NBC warfare exercise in central Tel Aviv. (IDF Spokesman)

and short-term intelligence-gathering assignments. The unit's sole mission was counterterrorism—it had no true conventional use, other than perhaps being deployed behind enemy lines, though the training each operator received was designed specifically for the Palestinian theater of operations.

Although made famous—or infamous as some claim—as a result of their infiltration and counter-terrorist operations during the Intifadah, Israelis have been disguising themselves as Arabs for nearly a hundred years in the unstoppable cycle of violence of the Arab-Israeli conflict. A *Mista'arev* is someone who isn't an Arab by origin, but due to various reasons dresses in Arab garb, acts in accordance with Arab manners and customs, speaks Arabic, and lives where most of the population is Arab. The term Mista'arvim is derived from the Arabic expression of *Musta'arvim*, meaning "intervening." Jewish Mista'arvim date back to 1909 and the "*Shomer*," an organization designed to provide security to the first Jewish settlements in Palestine. *Shomer* guards rode Arabian horses, dressed in traditional Arab garments, and learned to speak fluent Arabic to not only gain the respect of their neighbors, and to find out what they were up to. The *Haganah*, the military arm of the Jewish settlements in pre-

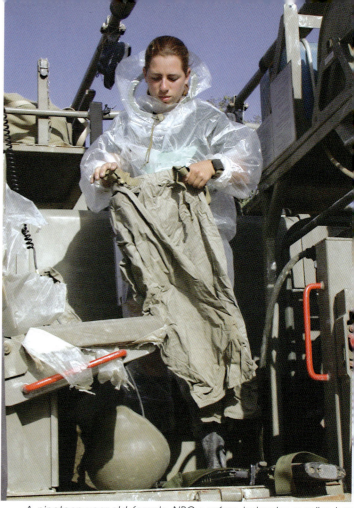

A nineteen-year-old female NBC warfare instructor readies her gear after training with a platoon of paratroopers. The threat of Hamas and the Palestinian Islamic Jihad has raised the level of awareness and concern among the IDF's chemical warfare specialists. (IDF Spokesman)

independence Israel, created its own Arabist intelligence unit during the bloody Arab revolt of 1936-39, when agents in Arab garb were dispatched to infiltrate local Arab villages. During the Second World War, a *Haganah* Arabist platoon called "the Syrian Company" was set up with British support to carry out sabotage missions deep behind Vichy lines in Syria and Lebanon. Most of the volunteers to this small, though unique unit were of Oriental descent—men whose families had come from the Arab Diaspora and who were fluent in Arabic and Arab customs. Commanded by Captain N. N. Hammond, an eccentric British intelligence officer and

Wearing a camouflage smock on his steel cover, a paratrooper takes aim with his M4 (fitted with a Trajicon sight) prior to embarking on a live-fire urban kill house in preparation for operations in the West Bank. (IDF Spokesman)

At a forward staging area in the southern portion of the West Bank, near Hebron, IDF armored forces prepare to deploy. Note the crews of these Ma'Ga'Ch MBTs carry the Glilon 5.56mm assault rifle—carried solely by armor and artillery crews. (IDF Spokesman)

*His hands dirtied from days of knuckle-scraping street-to-street, house-to-house, and even room-to-room combat, a young red beret from the 35th Paratroop Brigade takes aim with his M4 on a doorway inside Ramallah that his squad his just about to breach. (IDF Spokesman)*

professor of Greek history at Cambridge, the Syrian Company received extensive small arms, sharp-shooting, demolition, communications, and hand-to-hand combat training, as well intensive Arab language, customs and culture instructions. Another "Arabist" unit was *Shachar* ("Dawn"), more a force of intelligence plants than commandos, who penetrated large work sites to gather information and recruit double-agents; they also opened small cover businesses and peddler stands at Arab markets to camouflage their activities. Many of these agents transferred to the Shin Bet and the Mossad, to carry out intelligence and special operations.

Yet Israel's first taste of undercover warfare in the counter-terrorist arena came during the bloody campaign to neutralize the Gaza Strip in 1970, when the Israel Defense Forces (IDF) formed of a small, though very active, unit simply as "Pomegranate Recon." Created by the rambunctious and controversial OC Southern Command at the time, Major-General Ariel "Arik" Sharon, Pomegranate would prove to be as revolutionary as they were decisively effective. Three years following the 1967 Six Day War victory and capture of the Gaza Strip from Egypt, Israel ruled the densely populated squalor in name only. Heavily armed terrorists openly carried their weapons through the streets and alleyways of the strip and its refugee camps, and bloody attacks against Israeli soldiers and civilians were daily occurrences. The mighty IDF, an army that only a few years back humbled the entire Arab world, could not conquer a few hundred hardcore terrorists. Pomegranate Recon was formed to change the

*An officer from Sayeret Tzanchanim gazes across a back alley in search of gunfire directed at IDF forces in Ramallah. Note the recon operator's CAR15 designated marksman system fitted with a Litton Aquila x4 night-vision device. (IDF Spokesman)*

equation. A small force of only a few dozen men, Pomegranate Recon was commanded by a visionary special operations officer named Captain Meir Dagan[*1] who realized that conventional means could never defeat an unconventional army. Together with a concentrated effort by the Shin Bet,

[*1] Today, Meir Dagan is the director of Israel's Mossad foreign intelligence service.

*A paratroop sniper tandem report on Palestinian guerrilla movement from a window in one of Arafat's offices in the Muqata, his Ramallah Presidential Compound. Note camouflage head covering, typical for all IDF paratrooper and infantry units. (IDF Spokesman)*

*Sniping in the most comfortable chair terrorist money can buy! A paratrooper sniper clutches his CAR15 designated marksman system while peering out of an office inside Arafat's Ramallah compound. His weapon is fitted with the Trijicon ACOG 4x32 day optical sight. (IDF Spokesman)*

*Paratroop squad and platoon commanders from a reconnaissance unit converge inside a Palestinian Authority office to coordinate security operations in and around Arafat's compound in Ramallah. (IDF Spokesman)*

*IDF Chief-of-Staff Lieutenant-General Shaul Mofaz (left, carrying the Micro Uzi) and OC Southern Command Major-General Doron Almog (right, wearing field glasses) tour the frontier along the Gaza Strip. Because of PFLP, Fatah and Hamas death threats, Mofaz receives a Shin Bet protective detail (note plain clothes agent armed with M4 assault rifle). (Nadav Ganot/IDF Spokesman)*

*On April 8, 2002, during the bitterly-contested street battles for Nablus, Golani reconnaissance elements move toward the center of town. (Emanuel Eilan/IDF Spokesman)*

Captain Dagan and his men became what they hunted—"When you are in Gaza act like you are from Gaza" was a unit catchword. Unit operators not only dressed as local Arabs, but even disguised themselves as terrorists, moving through populated areas clutching Soviet-made assault rifles. They infiltrated the terrorists' world by eating in their restaurants, shopping in their markets, even staking out their whore houses. They made the terrorists uneasy and unsure of their own backyard—never to know who to trust, where to walk, and when they'll be attacked. In one year, "Pomegranate Recon" crushed the terrorist uprising in Gaza. They killed those who were armed (and some who weren't), destroyed intelligence networks, and blew up safe houses and arms caches.

Pomegranate Recon brought a subdued peace to Gaza that lasted until the eruption of the Intifadah in December when, once again, an undercover campaign to combat terrorism was needed by an army unwilling to use oppressive force and an enemy unwilling to be humbled by anything less.

Even before the Palestinian uprising began, Major-General Ehud Barak, then OC Central Command and today leader of the Labor Party, felt that the IDF needed a special operations element inside the territories. In early 1987, months before the outbreak of the Intifadah, Barak authorized the establishment of an undercover unit, to be known as "Cherry," that would operate in the West Bank as a covert intelligence and strike force. The first soldiers in the unit, all volunteers, were graduates of the Paratroop Brigade's squad commanders' course, and were later given a complete undercover instruction regimen including a "disguise course," counter-terrorist training, and intensive instruction in Arabic and Palestinian customs. A second undercover unit, responsible for the Gaza Strip, was formed a year later at the height of the uprising. Because of the difficulty in apprehending known and wanted terrorists in an area as dense and ripe for violence as the Gaza Strip, a struggle of what was considered biblical proportions, that Arabist unit would be known as "Samson," after the biblical hero who fought the Philistines in Gaza.

From 1988 to 1995, there wasn't a unit in the IDF as busy as the two undercover squads. They deployed daily, and nightly, for ambushes, intelligence-gathering forays and arrests. The list of fugitive and known terrorists wanted in 1990, for example, included hundreds of names in the

*A female operator takes aim with her M16 as she protects a frontier area along the West Bank during "Operation Defensive Shield." (IDF Spokesman)*

*A paratrooper searches the home of a Palestinian Authority official in search of weapons and intelligence material. (IDF Spokesman)*

*During the initial fighting in and around the outskirts of Jenin, paratroopers uncovered weapons and ammunition from a clinic. (IDF Spokesman)*

West Bank alone—by 1993, only a few dozen names remained on "West Bank's Most Wanted." Many terrorists preferred to surrender to security forces, or escape to Jordan and Egypt rather than find themselves behind the crosshairs of an undercover soldier's weapon. According to one Israeli human rights group, nearly 200 Palestinians have been killed in undercover unit ambushes, including some of the most dangerous—and fanatic—Hamas operatives the IDF has ever faced in battle.

In the zenith of their operational existence, the undercover units accomplished exactly what they were set out to do—inflict insecurity among the men wanted for terrorist actions, and, by blending in with the local landscape, becoming an invisible set of eyes and ears on a hostile arena. Wanted terrorists never felt safe on the streets of Gaza, Ramallah or Hebron because they never knew which face in the crowd was covered by theatrical make-up. Was the old woman with the groceries actually a twenty-year-old sergeant with an Uzi? Was the old-man with a cane and the unkempt beard preparing pounce out of his crippled walk to produce a gun and a set of handcuffs.

Unlike most other IDF special forces units, where instruction can last as long as twenty to twenty-four months, *Duvdevan* operators undergo an intensive training curriculum that lasts only fifteen months and includes: four months of basic infantry instruction; three months of advanced infantry training; two months urban combat instruction; five weeks advanced counterterrorism course at the IDF's world-famous Counterterrorist Warfare School; one month advanced unit counterterrorist training; and, an intense and highly-involved "Arabization" course where the operators-to-be learn basic and conversation Arabic, as well as intimate details of Palestinian culture. In this stage of the instruction the operators also learn the art of masquerade, and how to apply makeup, costumes, and even immerse themselves in the nuances of the Palestinian people. *Duvdevan*'s instruction culminates with a one-month sniping, driving, martial arts, and advanced squad leaders instruction.

Another of the IDF's specialized special operations units operating on a frequent basis inside the West Bank was "*Oketz*," a combined counterterrorist and search-and-rescue K-9 unit. *Oketz* is an independent formation, not assigned to any larger command, and receives its orders directly from the IDF General Staff. The unit is divided into five section—attack, explosives, pursuit, search-and-rescue, and weapons recovery. The primary dogs deployed by the unit are German Shepherds and Belgian Shepherds and Malinois; Bloodhounds are used for recovery, and Rottweillers have been used on certain special missions, such as in "Operation Brown and Blue" in southern Lebanon when *Oketz*, attached to a combined Flotilla 13 and Golani task force, deployed exploding Rottweillers to assault a series of underground caves in southern Lebanon.

*Reconnaissance paratroopers sift through M16s, ammunition and mortar rounds seized from a revenue office inside Arafat's Ramallah compound. (IDF Spokesman)*

*Oketz* was a particularly useful tool against terrorists since the Palestinians inherently disdained dogs—hardcore Hamas and Jihad operatives would routinely surrender to a pack of pursuing canines in absolute fright, whereas they would fight to the death if confronted by Israeli troopers.

Both *Duvdevan* and *Oketz* were ideally suited to hunt down many of the men who topped the IDF's Most Wanted list, though a large-scale operation required that territory be captured and towns—along with their

*During a progressive gun battle with Arafat policemen and Hamas terrorists in Ramallah, paratroopers seek cover as they push on and advance into the lethal labyrinth of a main thoroughfare near the city center. (IDF Spokesman)*

Weapons captured by paratroopers in the Muqata—Arafat's presidential compound in Ramallah. Weapons such as the RPGs were strictly forbidden under the diplomatic accords reached by Arafat and successive Israeli governments. (IDF Spokesman)

inhabitants—tightly secured. That would be the work of the IDF's airborne and infantry forces.

There are "four" infantry brigades in the IDF's Order of Battle—each one consists of a reconnaissance company, an antitank company, an engineering company, and a signal company. The 35th Paratroop Brigade is considered the elite of the four brigades; the *Tzanhanim*, as the paras are known, are the IDF's premier ground force. The IDF's elite pure infantry force is the 1st Golani Brigade—the battled-honored brown berets who have left their mark of courage and intrepidness in all of Israel's wars; highly-mechanized, the unit fields a fleet of M113 and *Achzarit* APCs. The 54th Giva'ati Brigade specializes in amphibious-landings and its sphere of operations is traditionally in Israel's south. The *Na'ha'l* (Pioneer Youth) Infantry Brigade (which fields one airborne-qualified battalion) is a highly-competent conscript infantry formation made up of soldiers who dedicate part of their military service to working on border agricultural settlements.

Of the four brigades, only Golani fields a fifth reconnaissance force—*Sayeret Egoz* is the counter-guerrilla entity within the IDF (the unit saw extensive operations against Hezbollah in southern Lebanon and then, in the West Bank, against Palestinian terrorist strongholds—primarily in operations against Hamas and the Islamic Jihad, though the unit did see action, as well, in raids against Fatah and al-Aqsa Martyrs Brigade strongholds.

The IDF's infantry, reconnaissance and conventional special operations units would not be the sole force entering the West Bank to hunt down those responsible for the months of terror; armor, artillery, combat engineering[2] and air units, would play an integral role in the assault on terror.

Any large-scale IDF incursion into the West Bank had to have four primary objectives: (a) the elimination of the terrorist infrastructure established and nurtured by the Palestinian Authority in the West Bank; (b) the neutralization of terrorist strongholds around Jerusalem (c) neutralizing Palestinian towns that facilitated terrorist attacks across the Seam Line[3]; and, capturing or killing enough of the masterminds behind the current wave of terrorism to seriously impair the Palestinian ability to mount future attacks.

Completely destroying the Palestinian terrorist infrastructure would be virtually impossible—IDF commanders knew—as it would require the Israeli military and security services to completely reoccupy the West Bank—and the Gaza Strip—as well as defeating, disarming and destroying the entire network of Palestinian security services, virtually 50,000 men under arms, that Arafat had put into place since the signing of the Oslo Accords. Any operation that completely destroyed the Palestinian Authority would be lambasted by the Israeli left, and, more importantly,

---

[2] The IDF Combat Engineering Corps fields two special operations units. The first, known as *Sayeret Yael*, is a demolitions unit tasked with select operations, usually behind enemy lines. Inside the West Bank, operating against a sophisticated and well-concealed terrorist infrastructure, *Sayeret Yael* was tasked with the destruction of arms caches and caves; often they were called upon to blow up booby-trapped locations, such as highly-volatile TATP labs and arms caches. For the successful safe rendition of large explosive devices, such as car bombs, vehicle devices, and other large-scale EOD work, the IDF deploys what is known as *Ha'Yechida Lesiluk Pt'zat'zot*, or Bomb Disposal Unit.

[3] The Seam Line is an indefensible invisible border separating Israel from the Palestinian-controlled portions of the West Bank. The Seam Line runs all along the northern tier of the West Bank, towards the western fringe, and to the south, around Jerusalem, eventually skirting near the Negev Desert. The most volatile portion of this unmarked and often mountainous frontier is the area nearest to the Greater Tel Aviv metropolitan areas, where cities such as Qilqilya, a Hamas bastion, sit only 300 meters from one of Tel Aviv's most affluent suburbs. A bit to the north, the Palestinian city of Tulkarem is only a ten minute drive from the seaside resort town of Netanya.

*In the outskirts of Jenin, in a basement of a house where some five small children lived, reconnaissance paratroopers and combat engineers uncovered a bomb factory, including 300 kilograms of the highly-combustible TATP, along with hundreds of kilograms of agricultural fertilizer and chemical agents. (IDF Spokesman)*

*The secrets from a Palestinian kitchen: a Palestinian bomb and improvised rocket factory, uncovered by IDF reconnaissance paratroopers in the Balata refugee camp. (Boaz Masika/IDF Spokesman)*

the capitals of the world—including Washington D.C., Israel's closest ally—since it would also mean the killing of Arafat. Militarily speaking, the operation would risk enormous Palestinian civilian casualties, and require an IDF presence in the territories for years to come; many inside the IDF's hierarchy viewed such a mission as impractical. As a result, when formulating a response to the Passover Massacre, and the months of suicide bombings that preceded it, the IDF was determined to fulfill the remaining objectives.

Ending the terror, especially in and around Jerusalem, was essential to any IDF West Bank incursion and ending the terror meant large-scale operations in an around Ramallah, Arafat's West Bank capital north of Jerusalem, and Bethlehem, the birthplace of Jesus, directly south of the Israeli capital. Much of Arafat's power in the West Bank centered on the *Muqata*, an old British Taggart fortress once used by the Israelis as their local military HQ, in the center of town. Destroying, or surrounding the *Muqata*, was both a strategic and symbol objective. Strategically, it would hold much of the Palestinian Authority's hierarchy hostage, confined to one singular location, making command and control of security service personnel and Fatah terrorists in the field, difficult. Symbolically, of course, there was great importance attached to behind Israel's plans to seize Ramallah and lay siege to Arafat's compound. It would physically minimize Arafat's stature in the eyes of the world and downplay his importance domestically, in the eyes of the Palestinians—especially as his Praetorian Guard stood helplessly by as Israeli armor ringed the compound.

Ramallah, though, was a labyrinth of terrorist activity that would be difficult to conquer. Some 10,000 Arafat security service militiamen were stationed in and around not to mention large numbers of terrorists from the Fatah Tanzim, the al-Aqsa Martyrs Brigade, the Popular Front for the Liberation of Palestine, and, of course, both Hamas and the Palestinian Islamic Jihad.

To the south of Jerusalem, in Bethlehem, the IDF would face similar strategic and symbolic objectives. Bethlehem, and its nearby village of Beit Jalla, bordered Jerusalem's southern suburbs—all that separated the two entities in most cases was an unmarked ravine or a row of olive trees.

*Bomb building components uncovered by Golani reconnaissance troopers in Nablus. (IDF Spokesman)*

*While fighting ranged in the West Bank during "Operation Defensive Shield," special operations counterterrorist strikes continued in the areas in and around the Gaza Strip. An EOD technician examines the working tools found inside a Palestinian Islamic Jihad bomb factory near Gush Katif. (IDF Spokesman)*

*Even though the IDF offensive in the West Bank was the largest military action in the area since the June 1967 Six Day War, terrorist attacks and suicide bombing attacks continued. On April 10, 2002, a Hamas suicide bomber blew himself up inside the No. 960 bus near Kibbutz Yagur in northern Israel, killing eight and wounding nearly seventy-five passengers. Police crime scene investigators sift through the remnants of that charred commuter bus. (IDF Spokesman)*

*A paratrooper antitank operator sifts through captured Fatah material during a late night raid on the home of an Arafat aide in a Ramallah suburb. (IDF Spokesman)*

Palestinians wishing to attack a target in Jerusalem—or anywhere in Israel—often had to do little more than walk across the unmarked frontier. Virtually every Palestinian terrorist group operated in Bethlehem and the UN-run refugee camps in and around the city center. The city would not be easy to conquer. Bethlehem was also one of the most Western of the cities inside the Palestinian Authority. Because of the city's biblical and historical significance as the true birthplace of Christianity, the city was the last—and slowly diminishing—bastions of Christianity inside the West Bank; the city's Christian centers maintained strong links with Christian centers around the world and the city, especially the area around the Church of the Nativity.

West Bank cities like Nablus, Hebron, Yata, Tulkarem, Qilqilya, and Jenin, would be dealt with last, as well as other villages and towns known to be hotbeds of terrorist activity. The IDF would face equally difficult military challenges—using infantry and armored units to hunt down terrorists hiding amid a hostile civilian population was never easy, especially considering the fact that groups like Fatah, Hamas and the Jihad had nearly ten years to entrench themselves well into the fabric of the city and its surrounding confines.

Operation Defensive Shield, Israel's counterterrorist offensive against the Palestinian Authority's infrastructure on the West Bank commenced during the early morning hours of March 29, 2002, when IDF armor units, led by paratroop and special operations reconnaissance units, broke across the no-man's lands separating Jerusalem and Ramallah. The advance was meant to be swift and decisive, and to reach Yasir Arafat's presidential compound before he could flee, or the men inside, the Palestinian Authority's top security and terrorist planners, could flee. IDF commanders expected resistance in and around the compound to be fierce. Arafat had long boasted that his Force 17 security force would fight to the death rather than allow the leader of the Palestinian people to come to any harm. When the first IDF reconnaissance paratroopers reached the gates of the *Muqata,* however, supported by Merkava Mk. III main battle tanks, Palestinian resistance fluttered. Small arms fire emanating from behind barricaded walls was quickly silenced by *Sayeret* snipers and the 7.62mm and .50 caliber machine guns mounted on the Merkava MBTs. The Israeli strategy was simple. Force those inside the *Muqata* into a series of rooms inside the main building, and destroy, in a symbolic gesture of humiliation, most of the palatial structure. Tanks crushed the vehicles parked inside the compound's immense lot; Land Rovers, Suburbans and other SUVs used by Force 17 were destroyed as were Mercedes, BMW, Toyota and Audi

*Mechanized Golani elements move into position near Beir Hanoun. (IDF Spokesman)*

*Two female soldiers, attached to the Paratroop Brigade's operations in Nablus, stand guard at their post, ready to repel any possible Hamas or Islamic Jihad attack. (Yzvika Golan/IDF Spokesman)*

sedans—many stolen from Israel—used by Arafat's top lieutenants. Two Mi-8 helicopters, painted white and green and used by Arafat to shuttle back and forth from Gaza and other parts of the West Bank, were also destroyed.

During the IDF's operations inside the *Muqata* compound, many weapons used against IDF soldiers and Israeli civilians were found, including material in offices and storage facilities directly in and around Arafat's office. These included:

- An RPG launcher
- Forty-three RPG rockets
- Two 60mm mortar shells
- Twenty-two AK-47s
- 1 AKM rifle
- Thirteen 5.45mm AK-74s
- Norwegian sniper weapons
- Three RPK light machine guns
- Four No. 26 grenades
- One Miller grenade
- One smoke grenade
- One No. 400 gas grenade
- 128 commando knives
- Two MAG action crates
- Thirty 5.56 action crates
- Three crates of AK-47 ammo
- Ninety-nine AK-47 magazines
- Thirty-five M16 magazines
- Eight 7.62mm magazines
- Five 9mm magazines
- Six short M16 magazines
- Eighteen combat vests
- Five bulletproof vests
- Twenty-four telescopic sights
- Five night-vision devices
- Binoculars

*Paratroopers negotiate the narrow alleys—ideal for booby-traps and ambushes—of Nablus in search of Hamas terrorists. The IDF's elite forces faced enormous difficulties in operating inside the choking confines of the Palestinian urban centers wary of inflicting unnecessary casualties or destruction to Palestinian life and property. (IDF Spokesman)*

*IDF Chief of Staff Lieutenant-General Shaul Mofaz poses for the camera with some female soldiers attached to the 35th Paratroop Brigade assigned to Nablus. The female soldiers, trained in all aspects of urban warfare, are full-fledged combatants in areas of operation such as Nablus, but they do not join their male counterparts on patrols and raids. (Tzvika Golan/IDF Spokesman)*

*Golani infantrymen prepare to move across an open street, seeking cover as they engage a Palestinian sniper, near Nablus, during the second week of "Operation Defensive Shield." (IDF Spokesman)*

*Close-up view of the M4/M203 system employed by a Golani infantry squad operating along the outskirts of the Balata refugee camp, near Nablus. (IDF Spokesman)*

Much of the equipment was in violation of weaponry and equipment allowed under the provisions of the Oslo Accords.

For four days, the IDF operated solely inside Ramallah. Elite teams of *Duvdevan* undercover operators moved through the town at night searching for a long list of wanted suspected that the Shin Bet and Israeli military intelligence had assembled. Teams of *O'Ketz* operators, moving swiftly to uncover terrorists from their hiding spots, rounded up wanted Hamas and Fatah operatives wanted by Israel for terrorist attacks both before and during the al-Aqsa Intifadah. Muslims have a cultural disdain for dogs—according to Islamic ethos, dogs are unclean—and many hardened terrorists seemingly willing to martyr themselves surrendered without incident once confronted by the unit's canine force.

Much of Ramallah had to be cleared neighborhood by neighborhood, street by street and even room by room. IDF units attempted to use as little firepower as possible to limit casualties to the local Palestinian population, but war—especially counterinsurgency warfare—is a dangerous and ugly affair. Palestinian terrorists hid behind the civilian population and often used men, women, and children as human shields. IDF responses to Palestinian firepower were often harsh and immediate. Palestinian civilians, tragically, were hurt and killed; property damage in parts of Ramallah was significant.

In Ramallah, Arafat's West Bank capital, IDF units encountered stiff resistance from heavily-armed Palestinian Authority security men, along with Fatah, Tanzim, Hamas, Jihad and al-Aqsa Martyrs Brigade terrorists. Once the IDF responded with armor, and teams of special operations unit, operating primarily at night, began to infiltrate into the neighborhoods where the terrorists ate and slept, Palestinian resistance waned. The commanders, cognizant that their names topped Shin Bet and Military

*M113s operating near Hebron. The IDF uses an indigenously-produced cupola and gunshield that consists of two sheets protective armor producing box configuration complete with bulletproof glass. (IDF Spokesman)*

*A paratroop lieutenant confers with the crew of an up-armored M113 near Nablus. The protective cupola was found to be incredibly effective in shielding vehicle commanders from small arms and sniper fire during assaults of major urban areas. (IDF Spokesman)*

*Intelligence officers assigned to the paratroopers display a forged Israeli license plate, used on 4x4s parked inside Arafat's Ramallah compound, to smuggle intelligence operatives and terrorists into Israel proper. (Roni Shizer/IDF Spokesman)*

*The terror of close-quarter urban warfare expressed on the faces of these young IDF paratroopers, clearing a narrow alley in the Balata refugee camp near Nablus during a sweep of Hamas activists near the city's notorious Kasbah. (Boaz Masika/IDF Spokesman)*

Intelligence "Most Wanted" lists, fled; these terrorist commanders, having stayed one step ahead of the bullet during Israel's controversial yet effective "targeted assassination" campaign (in which known terrorist commanders were assassinated), knew that survival required that they remain on the run.[*4] During the Israeli operation, dozens of arms caches were uncovered, and several TATP explosive labs were discovered—kitchens transformed into round-the-clock factories for the material that suicide bombers would eventually wear around their wastes.

By April 2, 2002, the IDF expanded the scope of "Operation Defensive Shield" beyond Ramallah when Israeli troops, supported by columns of armor, moved into Qilqilya, Tulkarem, Nablus, in and around Hebron, and Bethlehem. Some of the heaviest fighting took place in Tulkarem, a major Hamas operations center in the West Bank because of the city's proximity to the Israeli coastal town of Netanya and its use, by terrorist groups, as a staging area for attacks against Israel; the perpetrator of the Passover Massacre originated in Tulkarem. The fighting in Tulkarem was, initially, quite fierce; armed gangs from the *Izzedine al-Qassam* Brigade, the armed wing of Hamas, proved true to their words when they fought a fierce—to the death—campaign against advancing Israeli forces. Some of the heaviest fighting of the expanded IDF operation would take place in Bethlehem.

In Bethlehem, advancing Israeli forces faced little serious military opposition—Palestinians known to be on Israeli "Most Wanted" lists escaped to hideouts immediately after the Passover Massacre, and many of the so-called martyrs who swore they would sacrifice themselves in the Holy War against the advancing Israeli military machine, disintegrated into disorganized resistance. Terrorists who remained behind in the city used the holy sites in towns, primarily the churches in the center of town, as convenient firing positions, realizing that advancing Israeli troopers would be hesitant about unleashing tank and rocket fire on Christian shrines. This Palestinian tactics set into motion a bizarre and bloody chain of events that became one of the most desperate political sagas of the campaign.

During the IDF's initial move into the city, Palestinian strike teams, acting in unison under a joint Hamas and Fatah command, began using the city's holy landmarks as safe haven firing ports from where they could launch RPG barrages and mortar fire against IDF units. On April 2, 2002, Palestinian grenadiers fired antitank missiles from the Lutheran Church; numerous explosive charges were also detonated near the church. The next day, Palestinian terrorists took over the Santa Maria Church and held a priest and a number of nuns against their will, hoping that Christian human shields would dissuade the IDF from harming them. Palestinian arrogance against the Christian holy sites continued the following day when armed terrorists, including many men wanted by the Israeli Shin Bet, took over the Church of the Nativity and Manger Square, one of the holiest sites in all Christianity, holding numerous priests hostage and threatening to blow up the ancient church if the IDF attempted any assault. The siege of Bethlehem was underway.

*Nahal paratroopers deploy outside a house in the Balata refugee camp near Nablus during a sweep for gunmen and suicide bombers. (Boaz Masika/IDF Spokesman)*

[*4] On April 15, 2002, over two weeks after the commencement of "Operation Defensive Shield," a task force from *Duvdevan*, acting on an intelligence tip, cornered the most wanted of West Bank terrorist commanders, Fatah Tanzim leader Marwan Barghouti, in a cellar only a few hundred yards from Arafat's besieged compound; they were supported by reconnaissance paratroop units and operators from *Sayeret Egoz*. Barghouti, who had been a savvy political figure using his Tanzim militia with great skill to win the streets of the West Bank, was behind dozens of terrorist attacks against Israeli civilians living inside the West Bank, as well as inside Israel's pre-1967 boundaries. Barghouti was also viewed by many Palestinians—and Israelis, as well—as a possible successor to Arafat; he had earned his stripes in street battles fighting for Palestinian independence (fighting that earned him a lengthy prison stay in an Israeli jail, as well), and he talked of peace and coexistence when confronted by journalists and left-wing pro-peace Israeli politicians, though on the streets of Ramallah, Nablus, Hebron and Jenin, he spoke of the liberation of Jerusalem and the end of the Jewish state. Israeli forces have been conducting a manhunt for Barghouti from the first moment that IDF tanks crossed into Ramallah; security forces had even occupied his Ramallah home to try and snare him. Because of his political clout, Barghouti, it is believed, thought himself safe from the crosshairs of an Israeli assassination attempt, though as "Defensive Shield" continued in earnest, Barghouti believed that he was a marked man. When eventually cornered by the IDF special operations task force, an Israeli general approached the fugitive, offering him water and assuring him that the gauntlet of armed commandos only meant to arrest him—not execute him. Without offering any resistance, a shaken Barghouti surrendered and was taken to a police station for formal arraignment and interrogation. At the time of this article's writing, Barghouti is currently standing trial in Tel Aviv for his crimes against the people of the State of Israel.

*An operator from O'ketz, the IDF's elite K-9 unit, deploys in the city of Tulkarem, along with his trusted partner, seeking explosives and fleeing terrorists. (Ra'anan Cohen/IDF Spokesman)*

*With a face scarred by exhaustion a Golani grenadier walks through an alleyway in Tulkarem in search of Hamas operatives. (IDF Spokesman)*

*Paratroopers embark on a deadly cat-and-mouse game with Hamas snipers operating in Qilqilya, the West Bank town closest to the greater metropolitan Tel Aviv area, and a hotbed of fundamentalist Islamic radical terrorist groups. (IDF Spokesman)*

For the next thirty-eight days, Israeli forces, including military intelligence and special operations teams, surrounded the Church of the Nativity, cognizant of the fact that nearly forty armed men, equipped with explosives and antitank weapons, were preparing for a last stand and possible destruction of the holy site. IDF negotiators worked diligently to talk out any Palestinian willing to surrender; lack of food, water, and toilet facilities made conditions inside the church absolutely intolerable. IDF snipers, including rifles mounted on remote controlled hinges with computer-controlled optical sights, hit any terrorist reckless enough to present himself as a target. The standoff was simple. Among the thirty Palestinians held up inside the Church of the Nativity were thirteen men wanted for serious terrorist offenses that Israel was unwilling to simply write-off; these men, Hamas and Fatah commanders, ordering suicide bombings and sniping attacks that left dozens of Israelis dead and hundreds wounded, and Israel wanted them behind bars. As the siege moved into May and the humanitarian situation inside the church grew more desperate, IDF commanders in Bethlehem feared that the terrorists, faced with a choice of death or imprisonment, would choose death and destroy the church in their own act of defiant martyrdom. The destruction of the church, many inside the Israeli hierarchy feared, would be blamed

*Paratrooper sappers prepare to blow up a Hamas bomb factory in Qilqilya. (Ra'anan Cohen/IDF Spokesman)*

*Wary of snipers as well as suicide bombers, paratroopers nervously check out every noise they hear inside a Qilqilya alleyway, using their M113 APC as immediate cover. (IDF Spokesman)*

permanent settlement with the Palestinians over final boundaries, control access to and from Gaza to the West Bank, this was seen as an enforceable compromise). The thirteen most wanted terrorists, the men the IDF had wanted to arrest, would be exiled abroad, to Cyprus and then permanent banishment in a European nation willing to host them. The standoff ended on May 10, 2002, when, under heavy IDF and Border Guard special operation unit escort, the thirteen men lifted off in a chartered aircraft to Cyprus. Inside the church, though, IDF investigators uncovered scores of weapons, explosives, and other booby-trapped devices rigged to detonate. Had Israeli counterterrorist and hostage-rescue units opted to storm the church, the likelihood of damage to the holy site would have been great.

Of all the West Bank towns earmarked for IDF military attention, Jenin, in the northern tier of the territories, was expected to be the most difficult to secure. Situated at the northern tip of the West Bank, Jenin was always a city that maintained ties to Arab, living in Israel as full-fledged citizens, who called Galilee and the Wadi Ara region home; one could literally walk from Jenin to the Arab town of Umm el Fahem inside Israel in less than an hour. With some 50,000 inhabitants, many living in refugee camps, Jenin was a hotbed of fundamentalist Islamic activity. Although Arafat's Palestinian Authority seemingly controlled the town, the city was run by both Hamas and the Islamic Jihad. Many of the West Bank's most dedicated—and diabolical—terrorist commanders originated from Jenin. The Fatah movement (and especially its military wing, the "al-Aqsa Martyrs Brigade," under the leadership of Abbed El Karim Awiss), was very active in the Jenin sector. Jenin was also the main center of operations of the Islamic Jihad organization for all of the West Bank. Hamas maintained an extensive operation in Jenin, perhaps the largest of the group's network in all the West Bank. For Hamas, and its links to Israeli Arabs in Western Galilee, Jenin was an important base of operations for suicide operations against Haifa, and Nahariya; the organization's Jenin operation was so extensive, that the cells in the city were even behind suicide bombing attacks in Jerusalem, such as the notorious August 2001

on the Jewish State regardless if they were the ones who actually lit the fuse. Therefore, any and all attempts were made to end the standoff through negotiations.

In a compromise that some in Israel found hard to swallow, the thirteen wanted fugitives would be spared imprisonment but would face permanent exile—twenty-six of the Palestinians would be exiled to the Palestinian Authority in the Gaza Strip never to be allowed to enter the West Bank to visit their homes or families (since the Israelis would, in any

*A three-man paratrooper sniper team gingerly peer across an alleyway in Yata, near Hebron, battling out with members of Arafat's Force 17 in the town's narrow streets. Note the team's sniper, armed with a M16A2E3 Designated Marksman system with all the accessories. Note the weapon's hand guards. (IDF Spokesman)*

*A Golani officer looks at two massive pipe bombs, found inside a cleric's home, that were to be used against IDF vehicles operating in Nablus. (IDF Spokesman)*

*IDF Chief of Staff Lieutenant-General Shaul Mofaz visits paratroopers and intelligence units positioned outside the Muqata, Arafat's lavish presidential compound leveled—almost completely—by the IDF at the onset of "Operation Defensive Shield." (Tzvika Golan/IDF Spokesman)*

*An operator from Duvdevan, seen here in full tactical kit, deploys near Ramallah in search of fleeing high-ranking Palestinian Authority officials, as well as Hamas and Fatah commanders, wanted by the Shin Bet and Israeli Military Intelligence. (IDF Spokesman)*

bombing of the Sbarro restaurant in the Israeli capital that left fifteen people dead and over 140 wounded.

Due to the proximity of Jenin to Israeli population centers, the city has served as a launching site for numerous terrorist attacks against both Israeli civilians and Israeli towns and villages in the area. If "Defensive Shield" was going to succeed, Jenin's terrorist infrastructure would have to be destroyed.

The IDF push into Jenin commenced on the night of April 2-3, 2002—the assault into the city was led by paratroopers (both conscript and reservist units), Golani Brigade infantrymen and armor and engineering elements. IDF commanders hoped that, like Tulkarem and Qilqilya, Jenin would fall without a serious fight, though they knew the town was a hornet's nest of terrorist activity. The campaign for Jenin was a classic display of the difficulties and dangers of built-up area warfare—a highly sophisticated military superpower, mechanized and supported by reconnaissance drones and helicopter gunships squared off against a ragtag army of highly-motivated fanatical guerrillas who know the urban lay of the land like the back of their hands.

Initially, the operation went well. Supported by the nonstop flights of Apache and Cobra helicopter gunships, paratroop and Golani units, as well as Na'ha'l infantrymen and combat engineers, swept through the city in search of terrorists, explosives and weapons. Armor was hampered from operating inside the concentrated city where main streets were narrow and alleyways impassable to most combat vehicles. Destroying the terrorist infrastructure inside Jenin would be the work of the foot soldier, the reconnaissance operator, and the sniper—especially inside the city's refugee camp. The Jenin refugee camp, controlled by UNRWA (the United Nations Relief and Works Agency) consists of a series of shanty structures and crumbling apartment blocks concentrated into a 600-square-yard rectangle of squalor. According to UN estimates, 13,000 people lived inside the camp alone; other estimates claim the population inside the camp to exceed 25,000 inhabitants. The various Palestinian Authority security services rarely ventured inside the camp—elements of Fatah, Hamas, and the Islamic Jihad were the rule of law inside the confines of the sewage filled streets and they often battled one another for control of

*An O'Ketz handler tends to his dog during a break in the hunt for Palestinian fugitives in Ramallah. (IDF Spokesman)*

*A paratrooper grenadier pauses as his platoon assaults an apartment block in Qilqilya. (IDF Spokesman)*

*A paratrooper watches carefully through the Trajicon sights of his CAR15 as a Merkava MBT patrols the streets of Beit Hanoun. (IDF Spokesman)*

*At a forward firing position near the Israeli frontier with the Palestinian Authority near the Gaza Strip, a young Giva'ati Brigade FN MAG gunner trains his faithful squad support weapon, a forty-year veteran with the IDF, on a series of barbed wire obstacles that Palestinian terrorists have attempted to cross so that they could attack targets in southern Israel. (IDF Spokesman)*

the area. Homes, alleys and cellars were fortified. Many were booby-trapped.

The IDF first focused its attention on the city itself and the outer peripheries. After several days of pitched battles in which IDF casualties were light, most of the predefined targets in the city had been neutralized. Dozens of explosive laboratories and weapon-manufacturing workshops were discovered and destroyed, the Palestinian Authority security system in the town left in shambles, and hundreds of Palestinian men, many on Israel's most wanted list, and numerous armed Palestinians were arrested. Shin Bet and Military Intelligence investigators discovered reams of evidence concerning terrorist planning and activity in the Jenin area.

But the early successes were misleading. In the months prior to "Defensive Shield" the IDF had mounted several operations against Hamas and Jihad targets in the city that met with stiff fanatical resistance. Jenin was a challenging target to assault—especially if minimizing civilian casualties was a primary concern of the offensive force. According to published reports, the elite of the elite of the IDF was in position to operate in Jenin—operators from the IDF/Navy's Flotilla 13, as well as other reconnaissance and counterterrorist forces. Yet one of the IDF's most effective tools in Jenin, as well as other urban areas of the West Bank, was the Combat Engineer's armored D-9 bulldozer—when streets were impassable to armor, or possibly covered by booby-trapped devices the D-9s crushed everything and anything in its path.

IDF commanders had focused much of their attention on the city and after three days of fighting, much of the town was secure. The refugee camp at first remained silent, but when Palestinian fighters realized that the Israel Air Force would not flatten the camp, they dug in; their determination intensified when they noticed that the IDF, in the effort to limit civilian casualties, was only sending in infantry teams to neutralize the city. The infantrymen, paratroopers and operators, faced a labyrinth of death and destruction. Palestinian gunmen repeatedly fired fusillades of heavy-machine gun fire against advancing Israeli infantrymen when hiding behind camp residents, hoping to draw the IDF units into prolonged

*The tunnel rats of Nablus—Golani infantrymen search underground cellars for possible booby-traps, weapons, and terrorists hiding out from IDF dragnets. (IDF Spokesman)*

*Fascinating glimpse into material seized by Golani reconnaissance infantrymen in Nablus, following an assault on the Kasbah. Of interesting note are the homemade zip guns, martyr trading cards, and improvised indigenously-produced hand grenades. (IDF Spokesman)*

*A Golani squad gunner tightly clutches his IMI-produced Negev 5.56mm light machine gun, watches the windows of a three-story building in the heart of Nablus, during mopping up operations. (Emanuel Eilan/IDF Spokesman)*

*An M113 from the 35th Paratroop Brigade climbs a hill on the outskirts of Jenin—from what promised, at the start, to be the toughest campaign of "Operation Defensive Shield." (IDF Spokesman)*

*Paratroopers, under sniper fire, warily move into the market place in central Jenin. (IDF Spokesman)*

firefights in densely populated areas. At just after dawn on April 9, 2002, a reserve reconnaissance force conducted a search-and-destroy foray when they were ambushed by Hamas militants. Children, playing in an alley, lured the paratroopers toward the kill zone when they said they saw men with guns in a nearby courtyard. The paratroopers, seasoned reservists with years of experienced in counterinsurgency in southern Lebanon, were cautious; reconnaissance paratroopers were the elite of the airborne, and their combat skills were second-to-none. But the paratroopers could not have known that Hamas had booby-trapped the entire surrounding area with explosive charges. When the recon reservists entered the kill zone, the Palestinians unleashed an explosive hell. Thirteen reservists were killed in the ambush; nearly a dozen more seriously hurt.

For the next eight hours, under protective barrages from Cobra gunships flying overhead, paratroop and infantry units battled with Hamas and Jihad gunmen to extricate the wounded reconnaissance paratroopers and to recapture the initiative in the battle for Jenin. Additional special operations units were also brought into the fray. D-9s and Merkava MBTs ploughed their way through what was left of the camp. Within days, Jenin was declared secured but the battle for the city had been the toughest of the entire campaign. Twenty-three of the thirty Israeli soldiers killed in battle died in Jenin.

Like "Operation Defensive Shield" itself, the battle for Jenin was marked by controversy. The Palestinians claimed that the IDF had perpetrated a massacre in the town, killing over 800 men, women, and children (some fifty civilians were killed in the fighting). The IDF refuted these claims, as did independent Red Cross and UN fact-finding teams.

"Operation Defensive Shield" ended in a slow and deliberate manner—Israeli forces slowly and cautiously moved back to positions outside Palestinian Authority command and control once commanders felt that the terrorist infrastructure in a given area was deemed humbled.

*Golani troopers remove the body of a Palestinian killed in the fighting around the Jenin refugee camp, during a brief cease-fire arranged by the United Nations (note vehicle in the background). Of interesting note is the development in the IDF's infantry load bearing equipment, especially for infantry units engaged in urban combat. (IDF Spokesman)*

*IDF military intelligence officers look on as supplies are offloaded from a Royal Jordanian Air Force chopper rushing humanitarian and medical supplies to Palestinian clinics inside the West Bank. (IDF Spokesman)*

*Prior to entering Jenin, operators from Sayeret Egoz, the Golani Brigade's elite counter-guerrilla force, hydrate themselves with recently acquired Camel-back systems. (IDF Spokesman)*

The desert fortification the paratroopers were to storm consisted of a series of bunkers on a hill surrounded by dunes. The fortification, the same kind that dot strategic roadways in the western Iraqi desert, was a formidable obstacle to an assaulting infantry force denied the comfort of natural cover. The IAF would soften the target—AH-64 Apaches would hammer the target with missile and cannon fire, but neutralizing the fortification required forces on the ground. That was the job of the red berets.

As the paratroopers deployed 500 meters away from the target, the cadence of the choppers flying overhead grew louder as the Apaches moved in on their mark. Only a spark was visible in the darkened sky each

Militarily, "Operation Defensive Shield" was a success. The IDF uncovered irrefutable proof Palestinian Authority President Yasir Arafat's involvement in not only the day-to-day execution of terrorist attacks against Israelis at the hands of his Tanzim and al-Aqsa Martyrs Brigade legions, but of his support and alliance with both Hamas, the Islamic Jihad, and even the Iranian-backed Hezbollah. During the military operation in the West Bank, the IDF confiscated tons of arms and ammunition, hundreds of vehicles being prepared with explosive devices, and scores of TATP and homemade explosive factories. More than 2,500 senior wanted terrorists of the Hamas, the Islamic Jihad, and the Fatah, as well as others, who masterminded suicide attacks, were arrested or killed.

The operation, and prolonged extensions of it from the summer of 2002 to February 2003, bought Israel *relative* calm. Relative calm, of course, is a unique expression in the Middle Eastern military vernacular. Suicide attacks continued, but the Palestinian terrorist infrastructure had been dealt a crippling blow.

**February 2003:** At a training field somewhere in southern Israel, a company of paratroopers are engaged in a series of nighttime live-fire exercises meant to replicate a large-scale assault on a desert fortification. After two-years of incessant counterterrorist operations against a suicidal foe so close to home, Israel's elite formations were preparing to meet the challenges presented by the next immediate enemy to loom on Israel's horizon—Saddam Hussein and possible war with Iraq. The paratroopers, deployed throughout the West Bank since the outbreak of the al-Aqsa Intifadah, had not been able to adhere to their rigid training schedule where the A-to-Zs of conventional combat were hammered home to young paratroopers prepared for the rigors of full-scale warfare. The paratroopers assembled in the desert were expert—by virtue of their experience—in the dangers and difficulties of urban and irregular combat operations, but large-scale exercises, such as maneuvers with armored and artillery formations, had been put on hold until the violence inside the West Bank could be dealt with. Israel's enemies were not confined to the West Bank and Gaza Strip, however. The paratroopers needed to be ready.

*Operators from Sayeret Tzanhanim move through an alleyway in Jenin, hunting down wanted commanders from the Palestinian Islamic Jihad. (IDF Spokesman)*

*Even though the IDF offensive to clamp down on Palestinian terrorist activity was an all-encompassing effort, suicide bombing attacks continued. Here, in Netanya, only a ten minute drive from Tulkarem, police survey the damage caused by a suicide bomber in the city's central vegetable market. (IDF Spokesman)*

time a Hellfire missile was launched; the shimmering bursts of light emanating from the Apache's 20mm cannon fascinated the young soldiers positioned in the sand. Gazing toward the fortifications, the paratroopers observed the darkened distance erupt into bright yellow and orange explosions—the heat, and sounds, of the explosions were evident in full force seconds later. Once the airborne barrage ceased, the paratroopers moved out cautiously. Walking briskly toward their target, the platoon commanders worked diligently while keeping their troops in position. Once the company was 300 meters from the target, the pace of the forced march turned into a well-choreographed sprint. At the 200 meter mark, the machine gunners opened up, peppering the smoldering remains of the fortifications with everything they had. Thousands of 5.56mm rounds ripped through the sandbag and wooden structures, turning the bunkers into fiery shards of destruction. Fifty meters out of the target, the machine gun fire stopped and the platoons, divided into squads with preset objectives, set out to enter the dunes, subbing as trenches, so that they could kill any "enemy" soldiers still alive. Live fire exercises, especially those at night, were risky business, but the paratroopers had to know what it was like to decimate a conventional enemy in the type of warfare the paratroopers excelled at.

Watching the entire exercise from a ridge above the fields of fire, battalion, brigade and divisional commanders gazed through night vision scopes and field glasses, monitoring radio traffic and supervising the fluid coordination of their troops in the field. The brass was pleased with the performance of the company, one of the best in the 35th Brigade, and pleased to have their red berets out of the territories—even if for a brief training respite. The commanders knew that, when squared against Palestinian terrorists in bitter battle, the paratroopers had performed very well. They had served as the vanguard in "Operation Defensive Shield" and had played a significant role in the termination and capture of over 2,500 terrorists. The commanders knew that the IDF's elite had once again served as the nation's cutting edge in one of Israel's darkest hours.

*Hamas suicide bombing attacks even after the end of "Operation Defensive Shield." On May 7, 2002, sixteen people were killed and fifty-five wounded in a crowded game club in Rishon Le'Zion, southeast of Tel-Aviv, when a suicide bomber detonated a powerful charge in the third floor club, causing part of the building to collapse. (IDF Spokesman)*

Operators from Duvdevan, the IDF's West Bank undercover counterterrorist unit, apprehend Marwan Barghouti, leader of the Fatah Tanzim near Ramallah. (IDF Spokesman)

Palestinian detainees near Hebron are offered water by the paratroopers who seized them. (IDF Spokesman)

IDF special operations unit and intelligence officers search a Palestinian terrorist after giving himself up during the siege of Bethlehem's Church of the Nativity. (IDF Spokesman)

May 10, 2002—three of the thirteen "hardcore" Hamas and Fatah terrorists who had been held up inside the Church of the Nativity is escorted by IDF MPs (note blue beret) and Border Guard counterterrorist teams to Ben-Gurion International Airport for a flight to Cyprus and permanent exile. (IDF Spokesman)

Standing in between rows of barbed wires concertina and high-tension security fencing, an IDF Military Policeman stands guard at a detention facility in southern Israel. (IDF Spokesman)

A Palestinian youngster, held hostage by Hamas and Fatah gunmen inside the Church of the Nativity, gratefully greets IDF special operations and intelligence unit officers and NCOs after escaping from the besieged holy place. Note IDF officer (center) with a Browning handgun holstered to his leg. (Ra'anan Cohen/IDF Spokesman)

Some of the thirteen Hamas and Fatah gunmen removed from the Church of the Nativity wait for their processing to be completed before being allowed to leave Israel—under heavy IDF special operations guard—for permanent exile. (IDF Spokesman)

An IDF Military Policeman escorts a Palestinian prisoner to a detention facility "somewhere" in southern Israel. (IDF Spokesman)

And the terror continued....operators from Duvdevan examine the smoldering ruins of a house in the settlement of Itamar on the West Bank, attacked by Palestinian terrorists on June 20, 2002, in a strike that killed a mother and her two children. (IDF Spokesman)

U.S. State Department DSS agents, CIA operatives and British MI6 agents escort four Popular Front for the Liberation of Palestine terrorists, the men responsible for the October 2000 assassination of Israeli Tourism Minister Rehavem Ze'evi, to captivity, in a Palestinian jail in Jericho, as part of a multinational settlement to end the hostilities sparked by the March 27, 2002, Passover Massacre culminating with Israel's assault on the West Bank. (IDF Spokesman)

A photo of what conditions were like inside the Church of the Nativity after Israeli forces searched the abandoned holy site for any terrorists holding out following the agreement securing the release of the thirteen men wanted by the Israelis. (IDF Spokesman)

During an IDF sweep of Hamas strongholds in Hebron, in June 2002, paratroopers uncovered this gruesome photo of the nephew of a Hamas commander among the family heirlooms. (IDF Spokesman)

*IDF paratroopers, crouching in the middle of Manger Square, display some of the weapons seized inside the Church of the Nativity. (IDF Spokesman)*

*IDF troopers embark on a NBC warfare exercise—fearing that one day the Palestinian attempts to mount a mega attack against an Israeli target, like the 9/11 attacks against New York City and Washington, might involve weapons of mass destruction. (IDF Spokesman)*

*Operators from Sayeret Yael, the Combat Engineer's elite reconnaissance unit, train in waterborne operations. IDF commanders realized, at the onset of "Operation Defensive Shield," that future operations against the Palestinian Authority's terrorist infrastructure would require a special operations emphasis. (Ra'anan Cohen/IDF Spokesman)*

*Operators from the IAF's Unit 669 pull in a subject rescued at sea. For operations where troops might be stranded under intensive enemy fire, such as in the center of a West Bank city, the IAF readies all of its special operations assets. (IDF Spokesman)*

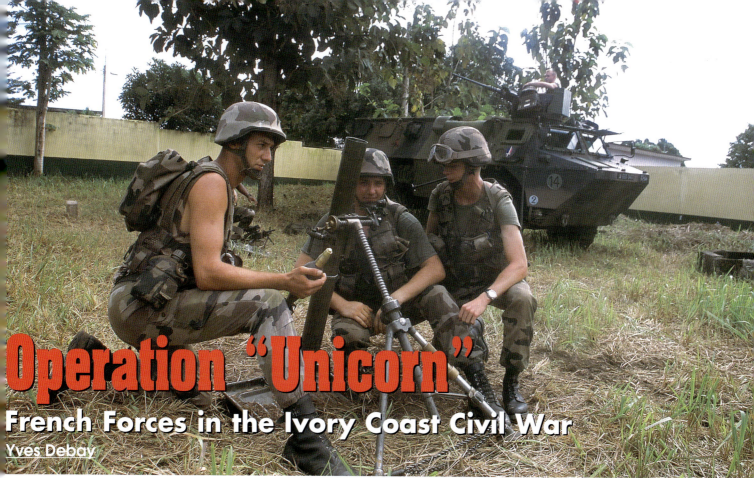

# Operation "Unicorn"
## French Forces in the Ivory Coast Civil War
### Yves Debay

*A mortar team from the CEA of 1st RCP man their 81mm weapon in Tiébissou.*

### Crisis in the Ivory Coast

The failed *coup d'état* that took place on 19 September 2002 has thrown the Ivory Coast into a civil war that threatens the stability of the richest country in West Africa. Though the coup failed in the capital city of Abidjan, the rebels, who are led by adjutant Tue Fozie, quickly took control of Bouaké, the second most important city in the country. It is difficult to say who is behind the rebellion, which is represented in the field by a cartel of former northern NCOs close to General Guei, who was assassinated during the coup attempt. The government of elected president Laurent Gbagbo has accused the neighboring Burkina Fasso of being the backbone of the rebellion. (One quarter of the Ivorian population are of Burkina or Malian origin.)

Officially, the mutiny and the subsequent fighting are a conflict between the northern and southern populations of the Ivory Coast. However, it is possible (though not proved) that the mutiny has the support of an Islamic country or maybe a terrorist organization. The control of the gigantic Catholic basilica at Yamoussoukro could be the goal of Islamic extremists. Curiously, the rebels are armed with 14.5mm KPV machine guns, which are not in the arsenal of the FANCI (*Forces armées nationales de Côte-d'Ivoire* – National Armed Forces of the Ivory Coast).

From the outset of the crisis, the government force exhibited the classic dysfunction of the African army: poor discipline, absence of efficient tactics, lack of fire control (half of the casualties during the Bouaké counteroffensive resulted from friendly fire), and a fear of the night. The majority of the soldiers involved in the conflict, though officially Christian, are animist in their beliefs, which interferes with the fighting on both sides. They carry charms (*grigris*) and magic herbs to protect them against enemy missiles.

On 10 October, the rebels took control of Daloa, the cocoa producing

*"Red berets" of the 2nd Company, 1st RCP patrol on a trail in the bush country east of Bouflé. The terrain lends itself to ambushes, but both the rebels and the FANCI know that a provocation of or a confrontation with the French Army would be detrimental to them.*

*Paratroops belonging to the 2/1 RCP ride in a Marmont light truck that was provided by the 43rd BIMa.*

*Paras from a combat section of 2nd Company, 1st RCP inspect a bridge. The Ivory Coast has relatively few important bridges. If this one, which is located east of Bouflé, were to be destroyed, a large part of the country could be isolated. The soldier in the lead carries a Minimi light machine gun.*

*These French soldiers were photographed during a patrol. They are members of the well-known 1st RCP (Régiment de Chasseurs Parachutistes), a unit created in Algeria in 1943 and modeled after the US paratroops. The unit was heavily involved in the winter campaign in Alsace in 1944, especially at Jebsheim where the young paratroopers stopped a large-scale German assault that was supported by Jagdpanthers. Sixty years later their spirit is still the same.*

capital and main source of wealth of the country, which is the world's number one cocoa producer. Three days later, the best FANCI unit, the Marine commandos, counterattacked and repelled the rebels 30 kilometers (19 miles) north of the city. The successful counterattack was probably made possible by the presence of French forces that created a security zone between Bouaké and Yamoussoukro, the political capital of the Ivory Coast. During the previous week, rebel forces tried to penetrate French Army lines but were repelled following a warning shot.

Despite this event, and the delivery from France of ammunition for the government forces, the Abidjan press criticized the attitude of the French. The southern faction would like to push the French forces to interfere in the conflict, but the defense agreement between France and the Ivory Coast cannot be applied to internal Ivorian affairs. On Tuesday, 22 October, a crowd of some 3000 youths tried to invade the barracks of the French 43rd BIMa (*Bataillon d'Infanterie de Marine* – Naval Infantry Battalion), but they were repelled by tear gas and water cannons.

On the first day of the crisis, the 43rd BIMa and a contingent of US Special Forces conduct an operation to evacuate western nationals from Bouaké and Khorogho. The 43rd BIMa consists of a locally based command and logistic company, a reconnaissance squadron and an infantry company provided by troops rotating from metropolitan France. These troops are represented by the 3rd Squadron, 1st RIMa, which was equipped with 12 ERC-90 Sagaies, and the 4th Company, 21st RIMa. Reinforcements arrive quickly from the garrisoned troops stationed at Libreville (Gabon), represented by two companies of the 1st RCP (*Régiment de Chasseurs Parachutistes*) and the support and

*Young paratroops of the 1st RCP take up a position near a large anthill. The 1st RCP is the last airborne regiment in the French Army to be professionalized. During the Cold War, volunteer conscripts of the 1st and 9th RCP (now disbanded) were involved in Chad, Somalia and Lebanon, where they performed well. Fifty-six soldiers of the 1st RCP were killed in a suicide truck bomb attack on the Drakkar building in Beirut on the same day the attack on the US embassy killed 200 US Marines.*

*A Peugeot P-4 vehicle belonging to the 2/1 RCP travels along a typical bush trail.*

*Some 12.7mm PGM Hecate and 7.62mm FR-F2 sniper rifles of the 2nd Company, 1st RCP are seen here on the roof of the airport at Yamoussoukro. From this rooftop position, they can be used to fire warning shots.*

reconnaissance company of the 2nd REP (famous Foreign Legion paratroopers), who were stationed in Djibouti. These troops are sent to establish a security zone north of Yamoussoukro. In Abidjan, the 3rd Company, 2nd RIMa relieves the 4th Company, 21st RIMa. More reinforcements arrive later with the 3rd Company, 8th RPIMa (*Régiment Parachutiste d'Infanterie de Marine* – Regiment of Naval Infantry Parachutists). Now there were 1500 French troops present in theater.

On 19 October, the mission changes when France agrees to establish a buffer zone between the FANCI and the rebels. This operation, which is given the code name of Unicorn (*Licorne* in French), would be under the command of General Bath and the staff of the 11th Airborne Brigade. Three Transall C-160s, and three Cougar, two Gazelle, and one Fennec helicopters are also available, as well as a frigate at sea.

The first lesson learned from Operation Unicorn is that crisis management can be resolved with French troops stationed in Africa; only the HQ of the 11th Airborne Brigade has come from metropolitan France.

### Operation Unicorn

The events that transpired in Abidjan on 19 September were no surprise to French military leaders. For several years, economic difficulties and internal struggles for power led to a slow disintegration of the "economic miracle" of the Ivory Coast. Nevertheless, the country remains a haven of peace, prosperity and stability compared to its Liberian and Sierra Leone neighbors. Due to the defense agreements, France maintains an on-site garrison, the 43rd BIMa (*Bataillon d'infanterie de Marine* – Marine Battalion). Apart from its important role in the local economy, the

*Precision firing often proves itself to be a decisive factor in African conflicts. Paradoxically, the sniper rifle can save lives on both sides of a conflict by neutralizing a vehicle at a great distance. It surprises and calms the aggressors while preventing potentially harmful direct contact.*

"BIMA", as it is known in Abidjan, remains a real guarantee for the 20,000 French and EU nationals who have settled in the capital of the Ivory Coast. The previous Ivorian president, Conan Bédié, declared to Jacques Chirac that "the presence of the 43rd BIMa has saved the Ivory Coast the cost of having a defense budget."

The battalion consists of one command and logistics company based permanently in Port-Bouet in the suburbs of Abidjan, as well as a squadron of ERC-90 Sagaie armored cars and a motorized rifle company. The troops in these last two units are drawn from rotating companies (generally provided by the *Troupes de Marine* – Naval Infantry attached to the Army).

*A sniper team of the 2/1 RCP keeps a sharp lookout from a rooftop. Such a position could be very vulnerable to a direct hit by a rocket, but in Africa the main mission is to show the flag, not to fight.*

*A Milan post of 2nd company, 1st RCP in position at the Yamoussoukro airport.*

*The firepower of the French Army, which includes a number of Milan firing posts, remains very dissuasive.*

*In position at the Yamoussoukro airport is an Eryx that belongs to 2/1 RCP. In the background is a foxhole with a similar weapon ready to fire.*

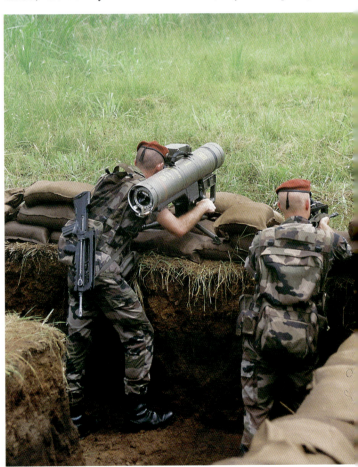

*This photo shows that the Eryx can be fired without a protective screen behind it.*

The missions of the 43rd BIMa can be summed up thus: representation of French military presence within the framework of the defense agreements, garrisoning of troops, training in the bush and in lagoon environments, and cooperative actions with the FANCI. Of course, the 43rd BIMa is also charged with evacuating French and European nationals during time of crisis . . . which is just what would happen.

On 19 September, the battalion is put on alert from the time of the firing of the first shots. Everything is ready from a military standpoint and at the Lagoon Commando Training Center everybody is on alert. (The particular geography of Abidjan, which is cut up by numerous lagoons, would require the evacuation of a portion of the nationals by barges or Zodiac rafts). In the rotating units – represented by the 4th Company, 21st RIMa and the 3rd Squadron, 1st RIMa – ammunition, food and fuel are loaded onto vehicles. In a few hours, the situation in Abidjan stabilizes and the need for a serious deployment is not required. A platoon is nevertheless sent on a stopover at the airport's military terminal.

As is usual in time of crisis, news coming from the north was both alarming and contradictory. Mysterious mutineers were descending from the north and heavy fighting had broken out in Bouaké! The opening of this front poses a real problem for Colonel de Kersabiec, the commander of the 43rd BIMa. In the urgency, it is necessary to organize for the protection and evacuation of the western nationals living in the north while still retaining troops in Abidjan. Paris promises reinforcements, but it is necessary to deal with the most urgent matters first.

Covered in tri-color flags, VABs, VLRAs and Sagaie vehicles dash down the Yamussoukro road. It is in this political capital of the country that they establish a small tactical headquarters for coordinating the evacuations. A convoy is even organized for Korhogo, more than 500 kilometers (311 miles) within the rebel zone. With American and French flags flying on them, civilian vehicles are collected and escorted in convoy by the marines toward Yamoussoukro where C-130 aircraft from the US Air Force are waiting. US Special Forces evacuate the American nationals who the 43rd BIMa have not already taken care of. A total of 3000 nationals are evacuated, 2100 of them from Bouaké alone. This brilliant operation earns laudatory comments from the famous American television channel CNN for the action of the French marines, which the *marsouins* (porpoises, the historic nickname for the French Naval Infantry) did not mind at all.

More than 2500 kilometers (1553 miles) away, deep in the jungle, the CEA (*Compagnie d'éclairage at d'appui* – Reconnaissance and Support Company) and the 2nd Company, 1st RCP (French paratroops) are at the shooting range at Ekwata as part of their rotation in the Gabon. It is there that the order of alert reaches the paratroops. "Light packs, one ration, arms and ammunition . . . and don't forget the paludrine (anti-malaria tablets)" are the only orders the NCOs issue; they are completely isolated

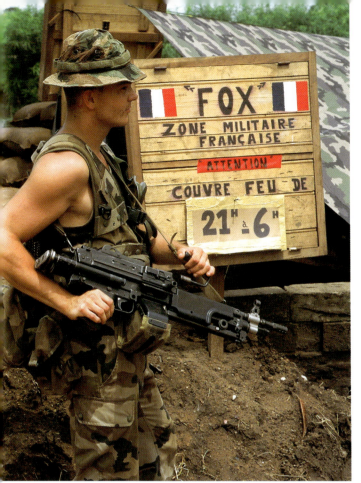

*For the sake of a good photograph, this soldier of the CEA of 1st RCP has put down his pickaxe and taken up his weapon. Having left Libreville in a rush, he is saving his unique dress for combat and is wearing a T-shirt to fill up sandbags and dig entrenchments. The temperature in the region can reach 32° C (100° F) with 75% humidity. While conducting an inspection, General Bath, the very strict commander of 11th Airborne Brigade (himself a former Legionnaire), was unhappy to see the paras in T-shirts.*

*A P-4 Milan of the CEA of the 1st RCP in position in Tiébissou. The layout of the city and the good visibility at the crossroads would enable the lethal weapon to take care of any vehicle that tries to infiltrate the safety zone. The African boys were very curious about the Milan system.*

arrived at the end of its tour, it is relieved by the 3rd Company, 2nd RIMa (which has the same scorpion insignia), who stay in the capital. The 3rd Squadron of the 1st RIMa also returned to Abidjan, but it left a platoon of Sagaie armored cars with the paras. The mission of this last unit is twofold. First, to protect French and European nationals from all danger, including risks inherent to combat. (A zone of protection would be created, as well as a "No Crossing" line. French authorities warn that troops will open fire after firing a warning shot if it is crossed). Second, to try to achieve a peaceful resolution of the crisis through dialogue.

The military disposition of the 1st RCP is as follows: Headquarters at the Yamoussoukro airport; 2/1 RCP and a platoon of ERC-90 Sagaies at Tiébissou; CEA/1 RCP at the airport, with a section on the Bouaflé road; and CEA/2 REP at the Baptist school of Bouaké, with a section at Brobo.

The arrival at Tiébissou of the 2nd Company, 1st RCP commanded by Captain Govys will remain in the memory of the young parachutists as a

from the world and know just as little as the paratroops. At the Montclar barracks at Djibouti, the same warning reached the Legionnaire paratroops of the CEA of the 2nd REP who are also on maneuvers in the Horn of Africa. An Airbus is already waiting on the overheated tarmac at the Amboli airport.

The trip would be less comfortable for the "red berets" of the 1st RCP. Two Cougar helicopters took them out of the jungle in the middle of the night to drop them at the airport at Libreville where two Transall aircraft are warming their engines. They soon head northwest to the pearl of West Africa, which is under threat of a mysterious rebellion.

At the same moment, the tactical headquarters of the 11th Airborne Brigade, which is under the command of General Beth, embarks from Toulouse. Seventy officers distributed among six cells activate the crisis command post, which was set up in the 43rd BIMa. "Practically all we have to do is switch on a light," a signal officer tells us. Operation Unicorn begins!

Far away in the bush, a tactical headquarters under the command of 1st RCP is set up in Yamoussoukro. At the beginning of the crisis, the "boss" of the regiment, Colonel Thuet, an old "Chasseur-Para", establishes his CP at Yamoussoukro's airport, which is shared by the forces of the Ivory Coast. "It's about the use of a platform, not about its control," an officer told us. Every night the FANCI troops on site assure the protection of an Antonov-24 and a Mi-8 that are used to deliver ammunition.

Once they arrive, the companies settle down in the zones assigned to them, which allows the "4" of the 21st RIMa to return to Abidjan. Having

*This 81mm mortar is an old model as it was pulled from the stockpile of weapons kept in Africa. The units in France are equipped with the new long-barreled version.*

*Troops from the GCP (Groupe Commando Parachutiste – Pathfinders) are transported on a P-4 4x4 vehicle. These special troops belong to the 1st RCP pathfinder group.*

*The pathfinders of the GCP of the 1st RCP could also be grouped with the GCP of another regiment to form an even larger combat group that would be directly under the control of brigade. Such was the case during Operation Unicorn.*

true adventure. One of them relates: "This time it's for real. We were driven north in Marmont light trucks from the 43rd BIMa. A few kilometers from the village, in the middle of the night, the captain has everyone dismount. Advance notice of a mortar attack. The rebels had captured three 120mm mortars from the FANCI and if they heard the engines of the trucks, they might have tried to spray the route.

"Our advance was impressive. Only the noises of the African night and the rustling of our footsteps disturbed the threatening silence. We expected to be ambushed at any time. Our furtive silhouettes skipped into the ghost town. My finger was curled over the trigger of my FAMAS. In total silence we took up our positions in the northern outskirts of the town. A little before dawn, the three Sagaie of 1st RIMa joined us.

"At dawn, the mutineers made their presence known and tried to infiltrate our position. We fired warning shots, but they continued to advance. The Sagaies then engaged the enemy with smoke and IL rounds. The final warning had an effect and the mutineers did not press their attack."

A non-confirmed rumor says that machine guns were also used and that seven rebels were killed.

At Yamoussoukro, the airport CP is also solidly held. Mutineers and FANCI are able to assess the firepower of the airborne infantry. PGM, Eryx, Milan, FR-F2, and 81mm mortars are all in position, with every approach to the airport covered by their fire.

Two Gazelles, one with a 20mm cannon and one with HOT missiles are also on alert. The 20mm-cannon Gazelle, having been engaged and hit with three small caliber bullets during the evacuation of the nationals, was forced to return fire . . . instantly silencing the unidentified aggressors. The belligerent parties respect the firepower of the French army. Even though it is not their mission (which is primarily the protection of Western nationals), the French troops plan to stabilize the front that exists in the center of the country. Though this unnamed intervention on the part of the French is a hindrance to the progress of the rebels, it also hampers the success of the FANCI.

In a P-4 (a 4x4 Peugeot), we follow Colonel Thuet, who is in Tiébissou to inspect the positions of the CEA, which relieved the 2nd

*An Eryx missile launcher belonging to the CEA of the 1st RCP is shown in position in a bunker at Tiébissou. Note the firing plan drawn in chalk in the background.*

*Two Cougar helicopters took part in Operation Unicorn, the aircraft come from Pau and belong to Special Operations Command. On maneuvers in Libreville, a door gunner sits behind a machine gun mounted aboard one of the Cougars. The 7.62mm machine gun is used for self-defense, not for the kind of support that a 20mm cannon usually provides.*

*One of the two Cougar helicopters employed in Operation Unicorn returns from Ndokouassikro, an area covered by the 2nd Company of the 1st RCP. In this particular theater of operations, a Cougar with a little potential and a stick of paratroops can work miracles.*

*The terrain in the humanitarian zone forces the EMT of the 1st RCP to scatter its sections of paratroops.*

Company. The officer views with satisfaction daily African life resuming its course. "At our arrival," he says, " there was fear that the authorities had [made a mistake]. But look! That market has just reopened!" Under the eyes of the returning townspeople, who are reassured by the presence of the French, the paras improve their combat positions. More than 30,000 refugees passed through the town. The stream of humanity has dried up, but pedestrians and vehicles are stopped and sometimes searched on the edge of town by the Ivorian soldiers.

Relations with the FANCI are neither bad nor good. The African style of fighting is disconcerting to the paratroops who are accustomed to tight management and strict discipline. For example, one time a Toyota filled with mutineers came speeding toward the "No Crossing" line. The corporal in charge of the Hecate PGM sniper team signaled the vehicle and, after receiving authorization, fired a warning shot. The big 12.7mm projectile slammed into the bumper with a thud. The Toyota crashed on the spot and two men got out with their hands up. They stayed that way for ten minutes before disappearing in to the bush. That same night, the FANCI who were manning their position encountered some of their own men retreating from Bouaké. Due to a lack of coordination, uncontrolled fire suddenly opened up all along the line. In turn, distant positions several kilometers away opened fire into nothingness. Dozens of projectiles passed only inches above the heads of the *chasseurs parachutistes*, obliging them to "hit the dirt." Because of their superstitious beliefs, many of the African soldiers are afraid at night and, to feel reassured, open fire at the least provocation.

In another sector, audacious government soldiers decided to mount a night ambush, and they warn the French troops about it. Unable to intervene in Ivorian affairs, the French troops acquiesced but indicated that at a specific time a logistic liaison would be made by truck at an isolated post. Of course, that never took place . . . and the French truck was ambushed. Only the cold blood of the crew prevented instinctive retaliatory fire and a catastrophe from occurring. It is always that rigid discipline that makes the difference.

In Tiébissou's northern outskirts, paras set up their positions. Some distance behind them, an ERC-90 Sagaie monitors the sector, its turret at the 3 o'clock position so as not to point at either the mutineers or the FANCI. Captain Demay, commander of the CEA, explained to us, "With the premature arrival of the rainy season, control of the country can only he achieved by a war of the roadways. The roads are beautiful and run in straight lines. Alongside them there are few passable paths, and vegetation and swamps prevent any turning movement. My company, although a little spread out, is able to keep hold of the route to Tiébissou, which is the northern entrance to our security bubble."

The important area of the humanitarian zone is the main preoccupation of Colonel Thuet, who sees his three combat companies distributed over a sizeable geographic area. Radio contact is sometimes difficult to maintain. More than 100 kilometers separate the CP from the 2nd REP, which has set itself up in the Baptist church east of Bouaké.

The Legionnaire paratroops have a ringside seat for monitoring the fighting at Bouaké. A staff sergeant, a Polish soldier in the service of France, told us: "The FANCI passed by here along the wall in single file.

*From the beginning of the crisis, the 3rd Squadron of the 1st RIMa supplied the armored contribution to Operation Unicorn. Here an ERC-90 Sagaie holds a position in the northern sector of Tiébissou.*

*Situated as it is in this photo, this ERC-90 armored vehicle can engage any target driving on the straight road to Bouaké. This illustrates the importance of the axes of roads that traverse the Ivory Coast. Sagaies used smoke rounds to repel the rebels' infiltration attempts at the beginning of the crisis.*

*With the exception of the T-55s that stayed in Abidjan, heavy tanks did not make an appearance in the conflict. If they had, though, the ERC-90 Sagaies could have easily destroyed them with its 90mm shells.*

Another column was to attack from the southeast. They fired a lot of rockets and mortar rounds and bravely attacked a hillside, without much imagination. A beautiful frontal assault. There was a moment of wavering when the two columns put friendly fire onto each other, but they managed to set themselves up south of the town, with certain elements progressing toward the center of town. They did not know how to plan for a second echelon and the rebel counterattack found them low on ammunition. Then everything fell apart."

Further east, the section of sharpshooters under the command of Lieutenant Soulie is well-entrenched in remarkable combat emplacements supported by logs and sandbags. The Legionnaires again show off their traditional building skills. To save his combat rations, Sergeant Eloi negotiates with a delighted inhabitant of the area for a local delicacy of chicken, rice and banana. Half-naked children shout as loud as they can, "Long live France! Long live the Legion!" It is just another typical day in Brobo.

*A Marine (marsouin) observes the rebel lines from the turret of a Sagaie belonging to the 3rd Squadron of the 1st RIMa. In the tradition of the French armored units, the vehicle has been given a name, "Bazeilles", which was a heroic battle (a defeat) during the Franco-Prussian War of 1870. During that battle, the French Marines, who were surrounded in a house in the village, fought until the last cartridge was used. Every year the Marines celebrate the battle at Bazeilles on the 1st of September.*

### The Mission Changes

On 17 October, in the CP of Colonel Thuet, the atmosphere is feverish. With the cease-fire going into full effect, Operation Unicorn is about to change. Its purpose is evolving from a humanitarian mission into one of observation and enforcement of the cease-fire. The French troops would be setting themselves up on the front line between the rebels and the government troops. The combat group from the 1st RCP gives up one of its companies of Legionnaires to a new tactical HQ led by the 8th RPIMa, which is created to cover the western part of the country.

We follow the column of troops of Captain Doucet, the leader of the CEA of the REP, along the road to Daloa. The crossing of that city, which the FANCI had recaptured a week earlier, is made in a somber mood. The government troops are obviously very nervous and are aggressive with the members of the press. Twenty kilometers (12 miles) north of Daloa, the convoy comes across a number of destroyed 4x4s. The Legionnaires can also make out some corpses in the tall elephant grass near a VLRA truck. The distinctive smell of death permeates the area.

At dawn, Captain Doucet goes to the bridge at Baoulifla where rebels wait to negotiate with him. His purpose is simply to point out respective positions on the map in order to avoid any misunderstandings. About twenty rebels, who have blocked the road with enormous logs, wait under the protection of a 4x4 armed with a 14.5mm heavy machine gun. Their weapons are mainly Kalashnikovs, apparently new. Also visible are a FAL, two RPG-7s and some PM-PPSh-41s. The conversation is cordial. The rebel leaders have the reputation of respecting the French officers, who they often knew from the missions when they provided technical military assistance.

*This French paratrooper was the bodyguard for the author while in the field. Armed with the classic FAMAS, he also carried a Beretta automatic 9mm pistol in a leg holster.*

*This heavy sniper team of the CEA of the 2nd REP at Brobo is equipped with the 12.7mm PGM Hecate sniper rifle. Its heavy concentration of precision weapons has always been one of the Legion's great trump cards.*

After the meeting, and true to their open policy toward the press, the two rebel leaders "Big Dia" and "Dio the Trigger" share a few words with the media. Big Dia, who carries an MP-3, tells us: "We are freedom fighters and true warriors. When we set up an ambush it is serious and we kill some FANCI. It is the Angolans – you can tell by the color of their skin – and not fellow inhabitants of the Ivory Coast who have momentarily stopped us. We have seen them in the trees directing mortar fire. When they pounded the villages, we pulled back out of pity for the population that feeds us."

### Disposition of Units

As of 25 October, the organization of Operation Unicorn was as follows:
- Brigade headquarters (11th BP) at Abidjan.
- Tactical combat group from the 1st RCP at Yamoussoukro, including the CEA of the 2nd Company, 1st RCP to the east and south of Bouaké and the GCP (*Groupe Commando Parachutiste* – Pathfinders) used as infantry at Bondoukou.
- Tactical combat group from the 8th RPIMa, including the 3rd Company, 8th RPIMa at Touba and the CEA of the 2nd REP at Banoufla.
- The 43rd BIMa CCL and the 3rd Company, 2nd RIMa at Abidjan.

The ERC-90 Sagaie of the 43rd BIMa mounted by the 3rd Squadron, 1st RIMa are distributed among the various units.

### Restraining the Rebels

Operation Unicorn calls for the rapid placement of units into the bush.

*East of Bouaké, Legionnaire paratroops of the CEA of 2nd REP observe rebel positions. The VAB, like 90% of the vehicles used in Operation Unicorn, was taken from the arsenal of the 43rd BIMa, as the symbol on the glacis indicates. As far as the staff is concerned, the storage of materiel in country increases the efficiency of African operations.*

*The sharpshooter section of the CEA has been reduced in size since the loss of the 120mm mortars and the abolition of the Milan section.*

Even if the operation has been expanded a bit, the disposition of the troops, including four companies of parachutists, is geared toward performing the mission since it is about controlling the roadways and observing the cease-fire.

In Abidjan, the economic capital, the danger is completely different. The city is a typical African megalopolis of three million inhabitants with an urban area surrounded by townships. The Ivorian *gendarmerie* (police) did not even hesitate to burn down the towns next to their barracks. In a recent mass demonstration, the population expressed support for Laurent Gbagbo, but only one in three inhabitants of Abidjan are of foreign origin. Everyone in Abidjan knows that in the city the mutineers await their hour and that caches of arms exist.

In the event that fighting takes place within the walls of the capital, the 43rd BIMa should be able to insure the evacuation of the 20,000 western nationals. It would be a tremendous task that would require the

*The Legionnaire paratroops of the CEA of 2nd REP were able to construct respectable combat positions in just one day. The African armies are not trained and do not have the will to build such shelters.*

*This photograph shows the ample field of fire available to the French Foreign Legion paratroops from their position. With the exception of the Milan system and mortars, the weapons used in Operation Unicorn are the standard ones employed by any French infantry company to engage the enemy at a range of 300 to 600 meters (330 to 655 yards), depending on the terrain.*

*North of Daloa, a VLRA belonging to the CEA of the 2nd REP passes by a rebel pick-up truck that was destroyed during an ambush. Apparently the fighting in the north of the "cocoa capital" was relatively serious by African standards. The countryside near this site was littered with dead bodies.*

arrival of new reinforcements and a recall of the units that were sent into the bush under Operation Unicorn. The arrival of African soldiers of Ecomog, who are charged with taking the place of the French troops on the cease-fire lines, will no doubt provide some relief to the headquarters staff.

While waiting, the *marsouins* of the 43rd BIMa take care of business. Among the troops are the soldiers of the 3rd Company, 2nd RIMa "Scorpions", commanded by Captain Guillaume. Most notably they guard the airport and the residence of the French ambassador.

With two sections of the 8th RPIMa and the CCL of the 43rd BIMa, the men of the 3rd Company, 2nd RIMa were ready for the events that transpired on 23 October. On that day 3000 to 4000 youths from the Movement of Young Patriots of the Ivory Coast demonstrated under the leadership of the hotheaded Mister Blegoudé. To contain the flare-up of violence, the *marsouins* were forced to use water cannons and tear gas to disperse the crowd that was trying to storm the gate of the 43rd BIMa's quarters. That very evening, calm had been restored and the people on the street criticized the young people for allowing themselves to be manipulated by leaders that blow both hot and cold.

*With no hostility between them, a Legionnaire paratrooper and a rebel soldier stand opposite each other on the bridge at Baoulifla. A lot of contact has been made in this area between the French forces and the members of the MPCI (Mouvement patriotique de Côte-d'Ivoire – Patriotic Movement of the Ivory Coast).*

The crisis is certainly far from being over. The intervention of the French Army while not solving the problem has definitely prevented the destruction of central power and subsequent chaos. It is up to the

*A French officer negotiates with rebels at the beginning of the cease-fire observation mission. Similar talks occur with the government forces, but the FANCI become hysterical at the sight of a camera and do not allow the press to watch the meetings. This is definitely not the way to win an information battle.*

*A Legionnaire communications team attempts to establish contact with a Transall aircraft at an abandoned airport in Daloa. Because of the vast distances between the various elements of the French Army in the Ivory Coast, communication between them was sometimes difficult.*

*Legionnaires of the CEA of 2nd REP disembark to take up a defensive position in Daloa. The Foreign Legion remains a formidable military tool for the French government to employ when necessary.*

*A P-4 4x4 vehicle and a VLRA travel in a convoy down a road in the Ivory Coast. The VLRA is a fantastic light truck for use in the bush. It can travel up to 3000 km (1863 miles) and has a tank that can hold up to 800 liters (211 gallons) of fresh water.*

inhabitants of the Ivory Coast to decide their future, whether it will be an escalation of an ethnic war or negotiation through authorized dialogue. As for the FANCI, the future of the country is in their hands. Any excesses in the north could result in the radicalization of the population and bring an end to the Golden Age in the Ivory Coast.

### A Tactical Victory

As regards to the French military, Operation Unicorn can be viewed as triumph for the notion of stationing troops abroad. The crisis was handled swiftly thanks to the speedy arrival of 5000 men from Gabon, 150 from Djibouti, 100 from France, and the 600 stationed in the Ivory Coast. The 43rd BIMa supplied all of the material and ammunition, including 12 Sagaies and six VABs. A parallel can be drawn with the British Operation Palliser in Sierra Leone where Her Majesty's soldiers were required to seek authorization from Senegal before making use of the grounds at Dakar.

On the tactical side, despite all of the budgetary limitations of previous years, the French ground forces were able to master air transportation, and they displayed exemplary coordination with the Air Force. The airlift of vehicles was successfully accomplished and runways in the bush were used, such as the one at Touba from which Transall aircraft operated.

The rapid placement of a joint command post in theater and its smooth functioning are also reasons for satisfaction. It was able to command troops isolated in the bush far away, in some cases a couple of hundred miles distant, without the distance being a major obstacle. The last word rests with Colonel Thuet who declared: "I am a happy commanding officer with happy troops. Unicorn has given us – apart from any military-political considerations – action and a good operation."

*A marsouin of the 3rd Company, 2nd RIMa "Scorpions" stands ready to fire a Cougar grenade launcher. The weapon, which is perfect for crowd control, can propel a variety of 40mm projectiles. The 40mm Cougar grenade launcher was put to good use on 23 October during the demonstration in front of the barracks of the 43rd BIMa. The Ivorian press made mention of the "echoing bombs."*

*Two marines of the 3/2 RIMa "Scorpions" patrol in the garden at the residence of the French ambassador. Here at the residence, by order of Ivory Coast authorities, opposition leader Allasane Outtara was sheltered at the beginning of the crisis.*

Another mission of the French marines is to guard the military terminal at the Abidjan airport. The French air force made immediate arrangements for the use of two Transall and a Fennec helicopter based in the BIMa during Operation Unicorn. Other transport aircraft were engaged to bring reinforcements from Libreville, Djibouti and metropolitan France. The Navy also made available a Bréguet Atlantic. The marsouins wear a dark blue beret with a golden anchor on it. Like the Legion and the paratroops, they specialize in overseas operations.

A Zodiac boat belonging to the Lagoon Commando Training Center, under the control of the CCL of the 43rd BIMa. In the background is downtown Abidjan.

The ALAT (Aviation Légère de l'Armée de Terre – Army Light Aviation) was involved in Operation Unicorn with two Cougar and two Gazelle helicopters. One Gazelle was armed with HOT missiles and the other with a 20mm cannon. The latter was hit during an engagement with hostile forces and returned fire successfully. Here the two Gazelles are re-fuelled at the Yamoussoukro airport.

The last unit to be deployed to Operation Unicorn was the 3rd Company of the 8th RPIMa. The paras of this crack unit are seen here during a patrol near Abidjan.

Rebel soldiers use a huge log to create a roadblock on the bridge at Baoulifla. These are the men Colonel Thuet met with after learning that the mission had become one of enforcing the cease-fire.

Rebels soldiers proved to be far more willing to have their photographs taken than were the soldiers of FANCI government troops. The weapons carried by the rebel troops of the MPCI appear to have been spared from the ravages of the climate indicating that they are either new or that the rebels have maintained them well, which is unusual in Africa.

This close-up photo of one of the rebels provides a good view of their typical dress. The author noted fewer charms or grigris on the weapons carried by the rebels than on those of the government troops, which indicates the presence of Muslims. Nevertheless, the latter group has animistic beliefs that have interfered with the fighting.

A "stolen" photograph of soldiers of the FANCI. Their dress indicates that they are an elite group. Unlike the rebels, the FANCI created difficulties with the press, thereby losing the battle for international information.

Since the beginning of the fighting, two Mi-8 helicopters have been used to transport ammunition to Yamoussoukro. Rumors floating about the base mention the arrival of two other machines of this type, as well as the delivery of a Mi-24. A Bulgarian contract employee pilots the machine shown here.

# 6 Jägerbrigade
## Austria's Gebirgsjäger
Carl Schulze

*During Exercise "Kristall 2001", two of the tasks of the Hochgebirgskompanie were to find weapon caches hidden in the high mountains and to locate snipers. Here a MG 74 team covers their comrades as they advance on likely hiding places of irregulars who are suspected of hiding their weapons in snow caves. Note how the MG 74 bipod is fastened to a wooden board. This prevents it from sinking into the snow. The soldier in the foreground rests his rifle on his ski poles laid on the ground for the same reason.*

*The Hochgebirgskompanie of 6 Jägerbrigade is unique in the Austrian armed forces since it specializes in fighting in high alpine regions. In addition to its special training, the company has specialized equipment. Here a member of the company is seen operating a GESAT satellite telephone during a reconnaissance patrol. Communications in alpine regions is a real nightmare. Satellite systems make the broadcasting of reconnaissance results quicker and possible, even over a longer range.*

The sound of eight incoming Bell 212 helicopters recalls vivid images of the US Army fighting in the deep jungles of Vietnam, but once the observer opens his eyes, he will encounter the extreme climate and wild terrain of a totally different environment. The wind produced by the rotors of the helicopters blows snow all over the place, and the temperature of –4°C (25°F) immediately drops to –20°C (-4°F) because of the wind chill factor. Special boards attached to the skids protect the aircraft from sinking into the snow as they softly touch the ground. Dressed in white camouflage suits, Austrian *Gebirgsjäger* (mountain troops) of *Jägerbataillon* 15 exit the helicopters. Wearing sunglasses for protection against the bright sunlight that can speedily damage their eyes, they quickly unload skis, rucksacks and other equipment needed for fighting in alpine regions.

We are in the Austrian Alps, 2350 meters (7710 feet) above sea level, where the *Gebirgsjägers'* mission is to take the high ground around the small village of Cathie, which has been captured by red forces earlier in the day. Even though the operation will last only a few hours, in the unfriendly region of low temperatures, snow and strong wind, the troops carry all the equipment they may need for survival in this environment. This is because the weather in the mountains can change suddenly. What may look like a ski holiday at one moment in the next moment can become a tough struggle for survival with lives being threatened by avalanches.

Soon after the helicopters are gone, the *Gebirgsjäger* troops put on their skis and move downhill to take positions from which they can engage the enemy below. By taking the high ground around Kühtai, the

*Here a member of the Hochsgebirgskompanie poses with night vision goggles, which he would usually only wear at night. NVG equipment works perfectly in snow-covered areas during the night since enough light remains to operate such systems. This enables troops to fight during the day and at night, but it also means they have to be ready to deal with the enemy 24 hours a day.*

*Gebirgsjägers are specialists in fighting in arctic conditions. Here members of the Hochsgebirgskompanie use their ski poles as weapon rests during a patrol. Because in deep snow it is difficult to fire from the prone position, often the only way the troops can get off a well-aimed shot is to kneel on their skis and use crossed ski poles braced by one hand as a rest.*

commander of 6 *Jägerbrigade* has gained a vital tactical position, and that is what war in high mountains is all about. Whoever controls the high ground can control the valleys and thus control the lines of communication and the entire region. The *Gebirgsjägers* of 6 *Jägerbrigade* are experts in operating in alpine regions, therefore the Brigade is Austria's core formation for mountain warfare.

### The Mission of the *Gebirgsjägers*

As an alpine state, Austria has 62% of its countryside covered by the Alps, with peaks of well over 3500 meters (11,484 feet) in height. The strategic defense plans of the independent country are designed to stop an aggressor in two ways. One is by stopping him directly at the border by slowing him down while moving through Austria by denying him use of the lines of communication through the Alps. In the event an enemy overwhelms the Austrian forces, they would conduct a guerrilla war in the alpine region, making the invaders' lives as unpleasant as possible.

Since home defense is the prime mission of all elements of the Austrian armed forces, 6 *Jägerbrigade* is well prepared for all types of warfare, with the bulk of its kit, as well as the training of its soldiers, being designed for combat in the high mountains. Often tactics in high mountains differ from that used on flat ground. This is due to the deeply cut countryside, steep cliffs and high peaks, as well as the scattered lines of communications. For the battalions of the Brigade, this means that if they ever deploy in total, they might often operate as individual companies scattered over a wide area, defending several passes in an area in which high peaks might be situated.

In the event of a deployment into an alpine region, each of the battalions of 6 *Jägerbrigade* will be able to control an alpine pass with adjoining crossing points or cover an alpine area 50-square-kilometers in size. Fighting in valleys and on the slopes is done by the heavier elements of the battalions, which are called *talstaffel* (valley force), while the fighting on the snow-covered higher regions and the glaciers is performed by the *bergstaffel* (mountain force), lightly equipped *Gebirgsjägers* equipped with skies and riding snow vehicles. The latter often have companies and platoons, and in some cases even sections, operating independently, which demands a high degree of leadership, tactical thinking and initiative from the leaders on all levels.

The helicopter plays a key role in modern alpine warfare. With the help of the helicopters, troops are inserted and extracted, reconnaissance patrols are moved into position, wounded soldiers are evacuated, supplies are brought forward, information on the enemy is gathered from the air, and heavy weapons are moved. Further, helicopter gunships provide fire support for troops during battle.

In addition to its wartime tasks, 6 *Jägerbrigade* must be prepared to support civil organizations (such as the Austrian border guards) in their duties. For the *Gebirgsjäger*, this means that they are regularly deployed along Austria's eastern borders to stop the crossing of illegal immigrants, drug dealers and smugglers. Another mission of the Brigade is to provide help in case of catastrophes, such as the avalanche drama that occurred in Galltür in 2000. Catastrophe missions mean deployment not only in Austria, but also everywhere in the world if the Austrian government decides to send Austrian forces on humanitarian assistance missions or disaster relief operations.

Last but not least, 6 *Jägerbrigade* should be ready to be deployed as part of international operations within the framework of the UNO and the

This soldier from the Hochgebirgskompanie is armed with the 5.56mm StG 77. He has night vision goggles mounted on his helmet and he wears the special operations vest issued to all members of the company.

A ski patrol from the Hochgebirgskompanie moves on to its next observation post in the high alpine mountains. All members of the company are expert in skiing. They use touring skis which, when fitted with special skins, can also be used for quickly moving uphill.

in light infantry skills, each specializes in a certain skill. *Jägerbrigade* 1 is the army's motorized light infantry brigade, equipped with the Pandur wheeled armoured personnel carrier. *Jägerbrigade* 7 is the airmobile element of the Austrian Army, equipped and trained to conduct large-scale heliborne operations. 6 *Jägerbrigade* is specially trained in mountain and arctic warfare.

With its Brigade HQ based in Absam near Innsbruck in western Austria, the Brigade consists of four battalions divided into twenty

OSCE. For the soldiers of 6 *Jägerbrigade*, this can mean a deployment with AUCON of KFOR, with SFOR in Bosnia, with the Austrian battalion of UNFICYP on Cyprus, or even with the Austrian battalion on the Golan Heights, which forms part of UNDOF. In December 2000, approximately 1180 soldiers of the Austrian Army, including personnel from 6 *Jägerbrigade*, were deployed around the world on UN missions.

### Structure of 6 *Jägerbrigade*

6 *Jägerbrigade* is one of three *Jägerbrigades* in the Austrian *Bundesheer* (Army). While each of these three brigades is highly trained

Troops from the Hochgebirgskompanie patrol in the high mountain regions. Note that they are linked with a climbing rope. This is an important preventative measure when operating in areas where avalanches might come down or where larger snow cornices exist.

Soldiers of the Hochgebirgskompanie are all well trained in skiing. During wintertime in the high mountains, skiing is often the only way to reach points quickly without using transportation like snowmobiles or helicopters.

*A sniper from the Hochgebirgskompanie poses for the camera armed with a Steyr SSG 69. Strips of white fabric offer some effective camouflage.*

*Armed with a Steyr SSG 69, a sniper of the Hochgebirgskompanie mans a position. Note how his "Ghilli suit" is made up of strands of white cloth that provide perfect camouflage, even in a totally white environment like this snow-covered slope. The snipers of the Hochgebirgskompanie usually operate in pairs. The second man acts as the spotter and is armed with a 5.56mm StG 77 assault rifle in case close protection is needed. Deployed at a pass in the high mountains that can only be crossed on foot, such a team can make it impossible for the enemy to pass.*

companies and located in eleven garrisons, which are structured as follows:

- *Stabsbataillon* 6 (HQ and logistic battalion): This battalion is divided into the Brigade HQ Company based in Innsbruck, a Signal Company based in Innsbruck, a Transport and Maintenance Company based in Innsbruck, and an Engineer Company based in Schwarz. In addition to these logistic assets, the battalion consists of two combat elements, namely the brigade's Reconnaissance Company and the *Hochgebirgs* Company, the latter being specially trained for fighting in high mountains.
- *Jägerbataillon* 15: This battalion is based with its HQ and logistic assets in Kirchdorf in northern Austria. One of its combat companies, 1st Company, is also based in Kirchdorf, while 2nd and 3rd Company are both based in Freistadt near the Czech border. The battalion's *Schwere Kompanie* (heavy company), with its assault pioneer platoon, a mortar platoon, a machine cannon platoon, and an anti-tank platoon, is based in Ebelsberg. The battalion is trained in all types of infantry skills. In addition to handling operations in mountainous regions, the battalion is the Brigade's airmobile-trained force.
- *Jägerbataillon* 23: This battalion is structured for operations in mountainous regions. Its HQ and logistic asset are based in Bludesch in western Austria where two of the unit's combat elements, 1st Company and the Heavy Company, are based. The unit's Heavy Company is identically structured to that of *Jägerbataillon* 15. Based at the battalion's second base in Landeck are 2nd Company and the battalion's transport animal platoon.
- *Jägerbataillon* 24: Having the same mission as *Jägerbataillon* 23, this battalion is equally structured, but has a third infantry company. The battalion's HQ Company, the unit's logistic assets, 1st Company, Heavy Company, and the battalion's transport animal platoon are all based in Lienz. The 2nd Company is based in Tamsweg and the 3rd in St. Johann.

In peacetime, the Brigade has a strength of some 830 professionals, mainly officers and NCOs, who train the 2500 annually drawn conscripts during their eight-month conscription period. In times of crisis, this strength will increase to some 4600 personnel by calling up reservists. As regards vehicles, 940 wheeled and special vehicles ranging from motor bikes to heavy trucks, including Skidoos and engineer machines, belong to the Brigade. The Brigade's 70 Hafflinger transport horses provide additional transport capacity.

In addition to 4900 small arms, the Brigade's arsenal contains 30 anti-tank guided weapon systems, 44 mortars and 18 machine cannons. 6 *Jägerbrigade* belongs to the 2nd Corps, which is based in Salzburg and is responsible for western Austria, with the regional commands in Oberösterreich, Salzburg, Tirol, and Voralberg. The second large combat formation of the 2nd Corps is the *Panzergrenadierbrigade* 4 (armoured infantry brigade). In times of crisis or during operations, both combat formations will be supported by the Corps' own support units, which

*Hidden from the view of enemy troops that have taken up a position in the valley, soldiers from Jägerbataillon 23 wait behind a ridge before going into action. The soldier in the foreground is armed with the 5.56mm StG 77.*

*Soldiers from Jägerbataillon 23 wait behind a ridge for orders to move. In addition to his regular kit, the man in the foreground is carrying a snow shovel, an additional kit mat and a UT2000 Akja rescue sled. All of this kit is needed if the worst-case scenario occurs and the soldiers become victims of an avalanche or another soldier is injured elsewhere.*

*Armed with a .50-cal ÜsMG, a machine gun team from Jägerbataillon 15 provides cover fire as their comrades advance. The soldiers wear white winter camouflage suits over their combat green uniforms. Note the large hoods that can be worn over the helmet. When deployed in such a fashion, one of the first live-saving steps to be carried out is placing the kit mat in position to prevent the soldiers from becoming victims of the freezing temperature of the ground. Under arctic conditions, sentries and other personnel need to be well protected against the cold or they can become victims of frostbite and exposure. In addition, note that the soldiers who have to touch metal wear gloves to prevent their skin from sticking to the metal, which quickly reaches freezing temperatures out in the open.*

include Signal Battalion 2, Reconnaissance Battalion 2, Artillery Regiment 2, Logistic Regiment 2, and medical assets. The Austrian *Fliegerdivision* (Austrian Air Force) can provide transport and combat helicopters, as well as air defense assets.

### Weapons and Vehicles

The standard weapon of the Austrian *Gebirgsjägers* is the 5.56mm Steyr AUG assault rifle, which the Austrian forces call the *Sturmgewehr 77*. The *Sturmgewehr 77* is carried by every soldier of the Brigade apart from higher-ranking officers and medical personnel, who carry the 9mm Glock 17 pistol, known as Pistole 80 in Austria. Snipers are armed with the 7.62mm *Scharfschützengewehr 69* sniper rifle. The machine gunners in the infantry sections, as well as some soldiers in each unit, are equipped with the MG 74, which is a 7.62mm version of the famous MG 42 developed by the Germans during World War Two. The MG 74 can be used on a tripod, the Lafette 74, which extends its range from 600 meters (1970 feet) to 1200 meters (3940 feet). With the tripod attached, it is called the *Schweres* MG (heavy machine gun). Also used by the infantry is the US-designed .50-cal M2HB machine gun, which is called *Überschweres* MG (ÜsMG, or extra heavy machine gun) in the Austrian army.

The 84mm PAR 69/79 (M2 Carl Gustav) anti-tank recoilless rifle is used on the section level and in the support elements of the Brigade, while in the anti-tank platoons, the RBS 56 Bill anti-tank guided weapon system (called PAL 2000 [*Panzerabwehrlenkwaffe* 2000] by the Austrians) is used. The mortar platoons in the infantry battalions are equipped with the 81mm *Granatwerfer* 82 mortar and the 120mm *schwerer Granatwerfer* 86 mortar. The 20mm IFIAK 65/68 (Oerlikon GAI-BO1) is used in the heavy companies of the Jäger battalions for low-level air defense and fighting against soft-skinned vehicles.

The 940 wheeled vehicles of the Brigade include the 0.7-ton Puch G 4x4 vehicle in countless hard- and soft-top versions used as command and liason vehicles. Trucks are used in larger quantity. Among them are the 1-ton 4x4 Steyr-Daimler-Puch 710 "Pinzgauer" along with its longer brothers, the 1.5-ton 6x6 Steyr-Daimler-Puch 712 "Pinzgauer", the 2.5-ton 4x4 Steyr 680M, the 3.5-ton 6x6 Steyr 680 M3, the 10-ton 6x6 ÖAF 20.30, and the 4.5-ton 4x4 Steyr 12M18. Light vehicles include the KTM 250 motorcycle and Bombardier Skidoos.

### The *Hochgebirgskompanie* – 6 *Jägerbrigade*'s Elite

While all three Austrian Jäger brigades are basically equally

*Soldiers belonging to Jägerbataillon 15 advance on skies. The soldier in the front carries a MG 74 on his back. Ski training is an important part of winter warfare training since skis or snowshoes are, in some cases, the only means of reaching remote areas in the high mountains.*

*Fighting under arctic conditions can be hard work. Mental pressure and physical strain are manifested on the face of this Austrian conscript who has spent the whole morning from 2 a.m. to 9 a.m. on an advance to contact that has taken him uphill several hundred meters into the skies. He is armed with the 5.56mm StG assault rifle and belongs to Jägerbataillon 15.*

*During Exercise "Kristall 2001", Jägerbataillon 15 played the enemy. This IFIAK 65/68 cannon of the battalion's heavy company was set up in a hastily chosen position during the battalion's advance to contact with the UN forces.*

*While advancing to contact on skis, a machine gun team armed with a MG 74 from Jägerbataillon 15 takes up a position.*

trained for operations in the frame of a peace support operation (PSO). In addition, during peacetime the company is tasked with training the leaders of 6 *Jägerbrigade* in all types of high alpine fighting. Future plans include preparing the company to conduct peace support operations over a 6-month period on short notice.

The motto of the company is: "To the limits and way beyond." It stands for the high spirit of soldiers in the *Hochgebirgskompanie*, their unbreakable will and ability to fulfil military tasks in high alpine regions where other units can't even go. In addition, it stands for the will of each

structured, 6 *Jägerbrigade* is the only one with a *Hochgebirgskompanie* (mountain and arctic warfare company) in its *Stabsbataillon*. The multi-fold mission of the company includes the following: reconnaissance in high alpine terrain; fighting in extremely difficult terrain, e.g., glaciers and cliffs; preparing paths in high alpine regions to enable the other units of the Brigade to follow; operating as a Special Forces contingent of the Brigade; conducting search and rescue, as well as combat search and rescue, in high alpine regions; being prepared to fight as a normal Jäger company in support of one of the Brigade's battalions in all types of combat; being

*Troops of Jägerbataillon 15 prepare to fire an 84mm Carl Gustav recoilless rifle, the standard anti-tank of the Jägerbrigade. The weapon has a weight of 14.2kg (31lb) and is 1130mm (44.5in) long. In the Austrian army, it is known as the Panzerabwehrrohr 66/79.*

*Sheltered behind the protection of a slope, troops from Jägerbatallion 15 gets ready to use the Panzerabwehrlenkwaffe 2000 (Bill) medium range anti-tank weapon.*

The Austrian Jägers use the Panzerabwehrlenkwaffe 2000 as their medium range anti-tank weapon. The weapon shown here, which belongs to Jägerbataillon 15, is being used to cover a pass road.

In order to support the attack of their Jäger comrades, soldiers from Jägerbataillon 15 prepare their 81mm mittlerer Granatwerfer 82 mortars for a fire mission. In wartime, each Jäger company fields two 81mm mortars as its own fire support. The Jäger battalion fields an additional four 120mm mortars in its heavy company. In peacetime, all mortars are grouped together within the heavy company to allow better training. The personnel are trained on both types of mortar so, depending on the mission, the company commander can choose which weapon his company will deploy.

soldier in the company to approach his limits and, through constant high-level training, extend those limits. The high spirit and standard of alpine knowledge is achieved by only accepting recruits with alpine experience, many of whom are volunteers. Soldiers of the *Hochgebirgskompanie* also have to pass a special medical exam, and only soldiers who pass it are accepted. Training is hard, and even during basic training soldiers are often required to live in high alpine terrain for several days, their only shelter being caves dug into the snow.

The company is organized into a HQ and logistic element, which also consists of a signal element, a medical asset, and a reconnaissance and path construction team. The combat element of the company consists of three platoons, each with four sections and a command element. For fire support, the company has its own mortar section with two 81mm mortars. The last element of the company is a sniper section consisting of four sniper and spotter teams.

In addition to the standard *Gebirgsjäger* kit, weapons and equipment include everything necessary for fighting in the high alpine regions. The company's inventory also includes anti-riot kit for peace support operations, Skidoo snow vehicles, special combat vests, climbing and ice climbing kit, all materials for establishing climbing paths in high mountains, additional night vision equipment, satellite communication equipment, and some other secret equipment.

A mittlerer Granatwerfer 82 mortar of Jägerbataillon 15 is seen here during a simulated fire mission during Exercise "Kristall 2001".

The Steyr-Dainler-Puch Pinzgauer is seen here in the 4x4 variant called the Pinzgauer 710. Like its larger brother, the vehicle functions as troop transport, supply vehicle, weapon carrier, prime mover, and command vehicle. The photo shows the 4x4 Pinzgauer 710 in its soft-top configuration with the tarpaulin removed. The pictured vehicle belongs to Jägerbataillon 23.

to fight as an individual. In the mountain-specialized 6 *Jägerbrigade*, six parts of this training will be carried out in the high mountains whether it is summer or winter.

Some of the basic skills taught include the following: weapons drill on the standard infantry weapons such as the StG 77, Pistole 80 and the

This Jäger from Jägerbataillon 15 is armed with the 5.56mm StG 77. Translated literally, Jäger means "hunter". Since the 17th century, hunters were recruited in times of war for special formations due to their shooting skills. These units were then called Jägerbataillon or Jägerregiment. During battle they were used for skirmishing, reconnaissance, and fighting in built-up areas and fortifications. During the two world wars, Jäger units were used more and more as normal infantry units, though light infantry units did survive. The Jägers have always been identified by an insignia of three oak leaves and green facings on their uniforms.

All leaders in the company are trained as instructors or assistant instructors in mountain and arctic warfare. Most of them are also qualified army ski instructors. Just to give one example of the company's abilities, its four sniper teams enable the company to control a pass for dismounted troops in high alpine terrain. Each sniper has a range of 800 meters (874 yards) and during operations they can also be deployed along with the company's reconnaissance and path constructing team to enable them to set up fire positions that offer wide fields of fire.

**Austria's Conscript System**

Currently in Austria each male has to perform an 8-month period of national service. Women may also volunteer for service in the armed forces. The bulk of the soldiers in the Austrian armed forces, therefore, are conscripts. They are led and trained by veteran professionals drawn from the ranks of NCOs and officers. There are two options for fulfilling the service period requirement. One is an 8-month period in one of the branches of the armed forces with a high degree of presence. The alternative is a 6-month period followed by several refresher exercises (usually 10-days long and conducted every two years) in a militia unit, which will total a service time of eight months. However, after they have fulfilled their conscription time in one way or the other, the soldiers are attached to a reserve unit, which in times of crisis might call on the man again to become a soldier.

The training of the soldier can be divided into two periods. The first four months consist of basic training and the second four months are used for formation training. Basic training teaches the soldier the skills needed

Dressed in their white snow camouflage suits, soldiers from Jägerbataillon 15 check a suspect vehicle and its driver at their VCP. While the soldier with the slung weapon searches the suspect, his comrade provides cover with his 5.56mm StG 77. Note how the soldier conducting the search stands aside from the line of fire between his comrade's rifle and the suspect in order to avoid becoming a human shield in the event the suspect tries to escape.

The Steyr-Daimler-Puch Pinzgauer is used in countless 4x4 and 6x6 variants in 6 Jägerbrigade. It functions as a troop transport, supply vehicle, weapon carrier, prime mover, command vehicle, and so on. The photo shows the 6x6 Pinzgauer 712 in its soft-top configuration towing a 20mm cannon. The 2.5-ton light vehicle, which has a payload of 1.5 tons, is powered by a Steyr 4-cylinder petrol engine that develops 87hp at 4000rpm. The vehicle has a road range of 400km (248 miles) and a high speed of 100km/h (62mph). The vehicles pictured here belong to Jägerbataillon 23.

The 6x6 Pinzgauer 712 is also used as an ambulance by various units of 6 Jägerbrigade. The interior of the vehicle has room enough to carry four stretcher patients or seated patients or a combination of both. The vehicle is fitted with a hardtop and air-conditioning system. The crew consists of a driver and a medical assistant.

MG 74; sentry duty; parade drill and introduction to military life and manners; basic air defense and anti-tank skills; basic engineer skills for all troops; field survival and living in the field; first aid; signal skills for all troops; physical fitness training; live firing; individual battle skills; alpine training (skiing in winter and rock climbing in summer). Alpine training for soldiers of 6 *Jägerbrigade* will be no less than two weeks in summer and another two weeks in winter. Normally, at least one night of the week will be used for field training during this period. In addition, once a month there is a three-day exercise. After the fourth month, the learned skills will be tested during a four-day exercise.

Depending on the placement of the soldier in his unit, during the first four months he might also receive training as a driver and have to earn a driver's licence. In the following two to four months after basic training, the recruit will undergo formation training, which will finally enable him to act as a member in a larger team and to function in his platoon, company and battalion. During this period, exercises of one or two weeks in length will take place that could well see the soldiers training on the brigade level. Each soldier will also learn the skills needed to lead a section when the section commander is lost for whatever reason. In 6 *Jägerbrigade*, this period is also used for intensive training in mountain and arctic warfare, as well as for live firing at section, platoon and higher levels. Training also begins in this period for long-serving professionals, i.e., future NCOs and officers will be sent to appropriate military schools. Once an NCO or officer is promoted to the lowest rank in his career, he then will start to improve his skills by taking special courses while working in his unit. Further promotion coincides with the finishing of courses, service age, and being selected for a certain position.

Special courses especially related to the *Gebirgsjäger* of 6 *Jägerbrigade* are: specialized alpine training, including ice climbing; *Heereshochalpinist* (specialized course for fighting in high mountains), *Heeresbergführergehilfe* (assistant mountain and arctic warfare instructor); *Heeresbergführer* (mountain and arctic warfare instructor); *Heeresskilehrer* (army ski teacher); and *Heeresflugretter* (search-and-rescue-qualified personnel for work in helicopters).

### History of 6 *Jägerbrigade*

Today's 6 *Jägerbrigade* was officially introduced into service on 9 April 1999 by the Austrian Defense Minister, Dr. Werner Fasslabend, and

The Hägglund BV 206 is one of several special snow vehicles used within 6 Jägerbrigade. Here a BV 206 fitted with a scraper blade is put to use as a mobile roadblock. Powered by a 6-cylinder engine, the amphibious vehicle has a maximum road speed of 52km/h (32mph). The 4.5-ton light vehicle has a payload of 2,250 tons and, in addition, can tow 2.5tons. There is room for six soldiers, including the driver, in its front compartment, while 11 additional passengers can be carried in the rear. The vehicle has a stunning performance and its gradeability on hard surface is 1000%, and on 1-meter deep snow it is still 30%.

The 120mm schwerer Granatwerfer 86 is usually towed behind a truck mounted on a trailer. If necessary, it can be broken down into smaller loads for men to carry or else transported on horseback in difficult terrain. The mortar is broken down into the barrel, base plate, bipod, accessories, and ammunition. The picture shows a schwerer Granatwerfer 86 of Jägerbataillon 23 being towed by a Steyr 680M 4x4 2.5-ton truck.

*The helicopter plays a vital role in modern alpine warfare in the movement of troops, re-supply and fire support. Here troops are dropped in a remote region at 2350 meters (7710 ft) during a counterattack of Jägerbataillon 23 in order to re-enforce Jägerbataillon 24 during Exercise "Kristall 2001".*

*Medics belonging to Stabsbataillon 6 evacuate an exercise casualty. In the background, the SAR helicopter is just landing. The treatment and evacuation of casualties was one of the key subjects practiced during Exercise "Kristall 2001". The training also included the treatment of refugees, which involved medical and psychological care. However, the pictured simulated casualty was a victim of an anti-personnel mine laid close to a UN checkpoint.*

has since been commanded by Oberst dG Herbert Bauer. The Brigade, which specialized in fighting in alpine regions, received a potent leader. Between 1995 and 1997, he was the commander of the Austrian special forces center. Oberst dG Herbert Bauer began his carrier as a Jäger officer. This, along with the UN mission experience he gathered during the UNDAC mission in Southeast Africa, provided him with the necessary skills to construct and develop a modern light infantry brigade capable of fighting all types of wars and performing peace support operations in alpine regions.

6 *Jägerbrigade* is one of the three newly formed Jäger brigades that replaced the old *Jäger* brigades. Since the 1992 *Heeresgliederung* (army structure), there have been twelve of them. Several times they were needed before they were operational, but they consisted of only a small cadre of troops and needed to be filled in by reservists. The reduction in size of the Austrian *Bundesheer* (armed forces) to 110,000 soldiers in case of mobilization, as well as the creation of more present forces, was the result of the fast-changing security situation in Europe and the growing involvement of Austrian forces in international peace support operations. The new type of *Jägerbrigade*, with its high level of present soldiers, allows for a quick activation and fast projection of force when needed.

However, 6 *Jägerbrigade* can trace his history back to the 1 October 1956, when it was first formed as 6 *Gebirgsbrigade* consisting of *Feldjägerbataillon* 21, *Jägerbataillon* 22, *Jägerbataillon* 23, and *Brigadeartillerieabteilung* 6. In addition to its own artillery, the Brigade then also contained some independent engineer and logistic companies. In 1961, *Feldjägerbataillon* 21 was renamed *Jägerbataillon* 21, and in 1978 the Brigade also changed its name to *Jägerbrigade*. Between 1978 and 1995, the Brigade consisted of *Jägerbataillons* 21, 22 and 24, the *Stabsbataillon* 6, and *Brigadeartilleriebataillon* 6. From 1995 to 1999, the Brigade was reduced to *Jägerregiment* 6 with the mission of training conscripts and preparing them for mobilization in times of crisis. At such times, the regiment would have been brought up to brigade strength by the drawing on reservists.

### What Next? – The Future of 6 *Jägerbrigade*

As we look at world's trouble spots, many of which are situated in alpine regions (or at least in mountainous areas), it is only a question of time before we will see 6 *Jägerbrigade* going for the first time on an operation abroad. Due to Austria's growing involvement in international peace support operations, it is certain that the Jägers will then have to put their military skills into practice in order to restore peace to the population of a war-shaken region.

Troops of 6 *Jägerbrigade* were almost sent on an international mission to the Caucasus, but when war broke out between Russia and Chechnya, this mission was cancelled. However, during the author's visit

*This picture of a Jäger from Jägerbataillon 24 shows a soldier wearing the so-called Kampfanzug 2 (combat dress 2) with Gore Tex waterproofs. Inside his field pack he carries spare underwear, wash roll, towel, tent sheet, mess tin, field cooker, and 24 hours worth of rations. His equipment consists of a belt, yoke, two ammo pouches, water bottle cover, combat knife, and respirator case. Under the waterproofs he wears combat trousers, combat jacket and field shirt. Inside the pockets of his clothing he carries ear protection, ID card, and first aid pack. He also wears identification disks around the neck. In addition, combat boots and a combat helmet of ballistic fibre are worn. For his 5.56mm StG 77, he carries four magazines of 30 rounds each in the two ammo poaches. Note also that a ground mat is attached to his pack.*

The picture shows a 120mm schwerer Granatwerfer 86 mortar of Jägerbataillon 23 in operation during a fire mission in alpine terrain.

This Jäger from Jägerbataillon 24 is dressed in the Kampfanzug 2 (combat dress 2) with Gore Tex waterproofs. Note the collector for empty shell casings mounted on the weapon. This is used in peacetime during exercises that take place outside training areas to prevent polluting the environment with empty casings.

to the Jäger brigade's Exercise "Kristall 2001", the unit demonstrated that its soldiers were ready to handle a peace support operation. They also left no doubt that if called, they will go and act in accordance with the motto of the Austrian armed forces – "Protection and Help" – to protect where others cannot provide protection.

### Exercise "Kristall 2001"

Between the 17th and 27th of April 2001, Exercise "Kristall 2001" took place in Nordtirol in the Sellrain area and the Oberin valley. The main aim of the exercise was to demonstrate Austria's competence in conducting military operations in high mountains. The scenario of the exercise, which was designed as a peace support operation (PSO), contained some portions where troops were used for human crisis management, such as during avalanche catastrophes. In the PSO part of the exercise, one main aim was to train the Jägers to conduct a PSO in a mountainous region with peaks well above 2000 meters. Looking at current regions of conflict throughout the world, some of them are situated at such an altitude, e.g., the Golan Heights, the Karakorum, Afghanistan, and the Balkans.

The "number one" man of a 120mm mortar team from Jägerbataillon 23 adjusts the heavy weapon for a new bearing and elevation during a fire mission. The steep outgoing and incoming angle of mortars make them the perfect fire support weapon in the mountains. However, fire control is difficult for the FOO parties since the scattered terrain in the high mountains often consists of countless pockets of dead ground where fire control is not possible. This is one of the reasons why every NCO is trained in guiding mortar fire.

*Here a mortar crew of a 120mm schwerer Granatwerfer 86 of Jägerbataillon 24 prepares ammunition for a fire mission. The combat load of the mortar platoon includes 600 fragmentation rounds, 240 smoke rounds and 120 illumination rounds.*

*Secured on a UT2000 Akja rescue sled, a simulated casualty is prepared for evacuation by a team of soldiers on skis. Note that the casualty is wrapped in his sleeping bag for protection against any additional hazards of the freezing temperatures, which even on a sunny day can drop well below zero degrees in the high mountains.*

the co-operation between ground forces and helicopters of the Austrian air force, re-supply of forces in the high mountains, medical support for troops in remote areas, and construction of lines of communication over alpine regions.

Exercise "Kristall 2001" was the final test exercise for the conscripts inside 6 *Jägerbrigade* before they were released from the army after eight

For the Austrian army, it was their first PSO training exercise at such an altitude. Only a limited number of armed forces in the international community are able to train in such an environment. The exercise scenario included the following types of training for the troops on the ground: establishing and operating checkpoints for persons on foot and for vehicles; re-enforcing and protecting checkpoints; providing human aid to refugees; transporting refugees; protecting refugees against ethnically motivated violence; and controlling and re-enforcing the "freedom of movement" granted by an international mandate. Other exercise aims were

*In spite of the existence of modern radio equipment, signalmen like these from Stabsbataillon 6 can be seen laying wires for telephone systems that are often more reliable and less influenced by weather.*

*An engineer from the engineer company of the Stabsbataillon 6 marks a mine that is hidden under the snow. Laying mines in deep snow is an easy task in wintertime. Once snow has fallen again, the mines are so well camouflaged against visual spotting that they can only be found with sophisticated search equipment or by time consuming probing. Note the small skull and crossbones on the marker.*

*After a soldier is "injured" by a mine during Exercise "Kristall 2001", a member of the engineer company of Stabsbataillon 6 searches for other mines in the area in order to mark a safe path so medical personnel can reach the "wounded" soldier.*

*This motorcycle dispatch rider of 6 Jägerbrigade is mounted on the gl Krad 250 KTM. The soldier belongs to Jägerbataillon 24, which acted as the UN force during Exercise "Kristall 2001".*

months of national service and assigned to one of the many Austrian militia units that form the core of Austria's home defense. Some militia units were involved in the exercise, as well as units from the Austrian air force and troops from the army's artillery, engineers and the medical service. Austria's most secret unit, the *Zentrum Jagdkampf* (Center for Special Forces) was also involved in the exercise. In total, 3500 troops, with 500 vehicles and 19 helicopters, participated.

The exercise was split into two sections. The first, which lasted from the 17th to the 22nd of May, consisted of units being deployed in training areas to sharpen skills such as skiing, live firing, helicopter drill, PSO procedures, and human disaster relief. During the second section, between the 23rd and the 27th of May, the exercise was moved into the open countryside and into the alpine region around the village of Kühtai where the troops put their skills into practice during a PSO scenario.

The scenario was based on existing situations, such as the Golan Heights or the Caucasus region, where a fragile peace exists between two warring fractions that are then kept apart by a multinational force. However, each side has enclaves in each other's territory, and violation of the agreements is part of the daily routine. During the exercise, the troops from 6 *Jägerbrigade* were forced to deal with peaceful demonstrators, stop an aggressive mob from seizing a checkpoint, and show force when, following some incidents, one side decided to return with force into the demilitarized zone.

*A member of the* Hochgebirgskompanie *proudly wears the* edelweiss *patch on his peaked cap. The* edelweiss *flower, the famous insignia of the mountain troops, has been worn by Austrian and German* Gebirgsjäger *since World War I.*

Here a 20mm IFIAK 65/68 cannon of the heavy company of Jägerbataillon 24 can be seen in position providing cover for a UN checkpoint. Originally designed as an anti-aircraft gun, the cannon is mainly used today to give additional firepower to the lightly equipped Jägers. With its effective range of 1500m (1640 yd), the weapon can also be used effectively against soft-skinned or lightly armored vehicles. Thanks to its relatively light weight, the gun can be easily lifted to positions on a slope or in higher regions by a helicopter.

Visible in the foreground of this photograph is the standard liaison and command vehicle of the Austrian army, the Puch G 4x4 cross-country vehicle. The Puch G is powered by a 5-cylinder diesel engine with a top speed of 129km/h (80mph). Behind the Puch G, a 1-ton 6x6 ÖAF 20320 truck may be seen. The ÖAF 20320 can be loaded with 10 tons of equipment. Both vehicles belong to the engineer company of Stabsbataillon 6.

A rear view of a 6x6 Pinzgauer 712 of Jägerbataillon 24, which played the UN battalion during Exercise "Kristall 2001". Crammed into the rear are six soldiers with their full kit.

A ÜsMG is mounted on this 6x6 Pinzgauer 712 of Jägerbataillon 24. The vehicle was seen at a VCP of the battalion during Exercise "Kristall 2001". Note that the tarpaulin has been totally removed from the vehicle. It is also possible to remove the tops of the doors.

This 6x6 Pinzgauer 712 belonging to the Hochgebirgskompanie was photographed at a VCP while a convoy of busses passed by. The crew's rucksacks can be seen stored inside the rear of the vehicle. Note the .50-cal ÜsMG mounted on the roll cage of the vehicle. The 2.5-ton light vehicle can carry a payload of 1.5 tons or a full section of infantry with their kit.

The Browning .50 M2HB machinegun is used by the Jägers as the ÜsMG. It is seen here in position on a Pinzgauer deployed at a UN checkpoint during Exercise "Kristall 2001". In the Jägerbataillons of the Brigade, each company can field three ÜsMGs, which are divided among the three platoons of the company. Within the platoons, three sections are equipped with the 7.62mm MG 74 and the fourth is equipped with the .50-cal ÜsMG.

One of the missions of 6 Jägerbrigade is to be prepared for peace support operations. Here soldiers of Jägerbataillon 24 man a UN vehicle checkpoint during Exercise "Kristall 2001", an exercise that was designed to test the abilities of the Brigade to perform such a UN mission in an alpine region. The soldiers wear the new Austrian combat helmet made of ballistic fibers covered in "UN blue" and body armor also covered in blue. They are armed with a 7.62mm MG 74 and a 5.56mm StG 77. Note that they wear issue sunglasses while on duty to prevent irritation by the bright sunlight, which is even more intensified by the reflection of the snow.

A soldier of Jägerbataillon 24, on duty at one of the battalion's VCPs during Exercise "Kristall 2001", watches the approach of red forces, which will soon enter the zone of separation and push the UN troops out of their position.

This photograph shows to good advantage the anti-riot equipment employed by soldiers of the Hochgebirgskompanie during Exercise "Kristall 2001".

This photograph shows soldiers of the Hochgebirgskompanie during anti-riot practice. Their equipment includes shoulder, breast, back and leg protection equipment, as well as an anti-riot shield and a long baton. For head protection they wear the newly introduced ballistic fiber helmet onto which a visor may be fitted. If the situation calls for it, a respirator can be worn as well. If peaceful operations such as merely pushing the rioters back should fail, the soldier can make use of his baton to emphasize his point.

Anti-riot training in progress. In preparation for a peace support operation, members of the Hochgebirgskompanie prevent a crowd of aggressive demonstrators from storming a UN vehicle checkpoint. The soldiers wear special anti-riot gear that includes leg, arm and body protection, as well as shields and batons. One of the missions of the Hochgebirgskompanie in a PSO might be to act as anti-riot reserves who would re-enforce UN troops such as the crews at checkpoints.

Insignia of the close quarter combat instructor (Militärischer Nahkampf Ausbilder) of the Austrian armed forces.

This picture shows the national badge worn by all personnel of the Austrian armed forces (top) and the badge of the Heeresflugretter (personnel qualified for search and rescue work in helicopters).

The edelweiss flower has been the symbol of the mountain troops since the World War One. In 1915, Erzherzog Joseph Ferdinand introduced the edelweiss to honor the soldiers who fought in southern Tyrol with a special insignia. Since then, the edelweiss has been worn by troops on patches and on their caps. The best example is the insignia of 6 Jägerbrigade, which bears the edelweiss as a symbol of its mission to fight in mountainous regions. The green background is related to the traditional color of the Jäger troops. The term Gebirgsjäger stands for mountain infantry, combining the word Gebirge (mountain) with the word Jäger (hunter)

Company patch worn by members of the Hochgebirgskompanie.

Badge of the mountain and arctic warfare instructor, who is called the Heeresbergführer in the Austrian army.

# The Devils of Bandit Country
## Irish Defense Forces EOD Teams and the 27th Infantry Mobile Security Group

Samuel M. Katz

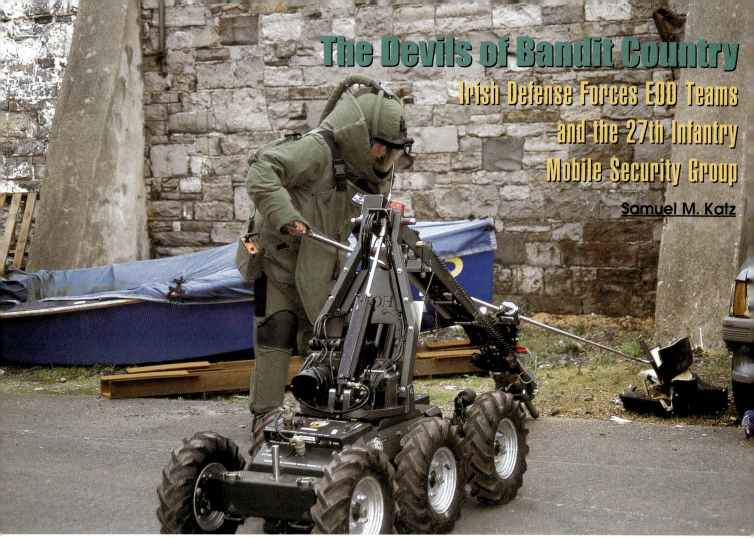

*If the Hobo's first disrupter round was not successful in rendering the suspect package safe, then the robot stands at the ready for the launch of another explosive round.*

Dundalk, County Louth—the Republic of Ireland. It is a typical winter's morning in one of republic's twenty-six counties. A howling wind sweeps across rolling green hills as the hints of frozen rain gently cascade down to earth. The overcast skies turn daylight into the deadened strokes of gray. Although there are no rows of barbed wire concertina, minefields, electronic trip wires or any other telltale hints of this being a besieged border area, Dundalk is a border town very much in the crosshairs of centuries of strife. Caught at the crossroad of what the locals simply refer to as "The Troubles," Dundalk is a town that touches the border separating the Republic of Ireland from the six counties of Ulster. It borders, in the north, the Northern Ireland county of South Armagh, long known as a hotbed for Provisional Irish Republican Army operations and coined as "Bandit Country" by British special operations forces engaged in a brutal guerrilla war in the hilly lawless county. Much of what reached the South Armagh in terms of weapons, explosives and other hardware of a guerrilla campaign has made it into Ulster through the cavernous, often unmarked frontier that is Dundalk. It is a major terrorist transfer point and a profitable smuggler's Mecca. It is, in the words of one intelligence officer in Belfast, "The gateway to Bandit Country."

*The Irish EOD "bomb truck" responds to a call near Dundalk. All bomb-disposal work in Ireland his handled by the military, though only the police can summon them into action.*

*At an alleyway in an industrial park near the border, EOD officers scan a discarded briefcase, believed to be a bomb, from the safety of fifty meters.*

With the supervising EOD officer already suited up and preparing his strategy in his mind for approaching the suspected briefcase, his team of support personnel ready their gear and the Hobo robot.

The "suit," the cumbersome hulking wrap of Kevlar worn by all EOD officers, offers the maximum of protection to the bomb tech tasked with manually approaching a suspected device.

Before rendering his decision if the device has been successfully handled, the EOD officer pokes the suspect briefcase with a specially-modified pole.

device of destruction is an obstacle to grander plans of carnage and is a coveted target. It might take the IRA or the Ulster Volunteer Force months to plan and execute the mere placement of a device alongside a military road, and it might take a bomb tech only ten minutes to successfully defuse that bomb. Therefore the terrorists have, in the past, made killing EOD officers their number one priority.

Along an agricultural road that brushes across the border, often crossing in and out of the two separate countries, on a muddied path favored by smugglers, a convoy of Toyota 4x4s and heavy trucks races toward a gully that borders both nations. The vehicles, all painted a dull olive drab, flash blue warning lights as they drive past shepherds wary of their flock and kids playing with their bicycles. A farmer walking his dog has discovered a box with wires on his properties. Anyone in Dundalk knows enough that a box with wires can mean but one thing—an improvised explosive device. Rushing to his house, the farmer called the *Garda*, the Irish Police, who in turn contacted the Irish Defense Forces EOD officer on duty at the army barracks in Dundalk. Yet in the bloodied landscape of the troubles, bomb techs are not afforded the luxury of plying their dangerous trade with impunity. They have gigantic crosshairs on their back and they require special forces protection. In Ireland, in Dundalk along the border with bandit country, the bomb techs use their skills and courage to walk up and manually handle an explosive device. Yet they rely on the commando-qualified skills of the MSGs, or Mobile Security Groups, to ensure their safety.

An old Irish prayer begins, prophetically, with the words "the peace of god is the peace of men." Yet in Ireland, both in the south and in the north, the peace of god and man has been shattered by a violent and turbulent history. The bomb has shattered the peace of god and man. Both the IRA and the Protestant paramilitaries target EOD officers in the Irish war of national liberation—anyone who can diffuse an intricately built

*With wires, battery and an enclosed substance believed to be Semtex, the bomb tech gingerly probes the contents of the briefcase so that the Hobo's second disrupter round can render the device safe.*

The *Óglaigh na h-Eirean*, or Irish Defense Forces, have played an intrinsic though completely unheralded role in helping to keep the Troubles from flaring into a conflagration fought in the south. They have patrolled the frontier, and used their special forces, the Irish Army Ranger Wing, to storm terrorist ships at sea. Yet the Irish War is a war of the bomb and the Irish Defense Forces EOD squads have been in the forefront. Explosive ordnance disposal officers in the Irish Defense Forces are considered among the world's finest and most experienced bomb techs. Besides their day-to-day duties of rendering safe terrorist devices throughout the 26 counties of the republic, they also serve in southern Lebanon as part of the United Nations Interim Force in Lebanon, or UNIFIL. In Lebanon, Irish Army bomb techs have handled some of the most sophisticated and, indeed, devious terrorist bombs ever built. "I thought our lads were creative," claims Commandant J.,* one of the EOD School's most experienced instructors, "but the boys in Lebanon, on both sides of the battle, are simply brilliant in an evil way." The experience gained by service at home and the bombers' ivy league that is Lebanon, military and police bomb disposal unit from all over the world come to Dublin to be trained by the Irish bomb techs at the legendary Clancy Barracks. But service in Lebanon, especially for an EOD officer, was a wake-up call in operational threats that were often faced at home, as the bomb tech never ventured to render a roadside bomb safe unless he was protected by a platoon of heavily armed infantrymen. Irish commanders realized that in Lebanon, where guerrillas will often martyr themselves, the threat of a suicide-attack on an EOD officer was a very real possibility. Counter-ambush and counter-sniper tactics were quickly developed by Irish troops accompanying EOD teams in Lebanon. Specially trained shock troops, equipped with heavy firepower and supported by snipers, would soon accompany every EOD call-out. Soon, identical standard operating procedures would be followed in the Republic of Ireland, where the men of the military's EOD squads are the last barrier between a terrorist bomb and scores of dead and wounded. "My primary job is to save lives," claims Commandant D.,* an experienced EOD officer in Dundalk, "but in the field I need the support of the heavily-armed infantrymen in order for my life to be saved."

In Dundalk, the job of safeguarding the EOD officer is the domain of the 27th Infantry's elite Mobile Security Group. Equipped with the Irish Defense Forces new speckled camouflage fatigues and the Steyr-AUG 5.56mm assault rifle, the twenty-man unit remains on-call, twenty-four hours a day, to accompany the EOD officer on duty to any call he will get. Each time the base's on-call bomb tech goes out on a mission—whether it be a suspect briefcase left behind in the washroom of a petrol station or a barrel-bomb, buried in the soggy moss, with lead wires heading back into the north—the Mobile Security Group will suit up, lock and load their weapons, and support the operation. "Out in the field, we will deploy before the bomb truck arrives with the EOD officer and his robot in order to create a tactical perimeter," claims Sergeant M.,* the commander of the 27th MSG. "Our troopers are trained to pinpoint locations where the terrorists, republican or loyalist, would place tripwires, booby-traps, and our counter-snipers are trained to search for possible sniper positions," Sergeant M. continues, "we place ourselves between the bomb tech and danger in order to allow him to do his job safely, properly and without having to worry about who might be looking to gun him down." If a threat is located and engaged, the MSGs are determined to eliminate any and all threats with decisive firepower.

To be able to meet any threat, including heavily armed Provisional IRA hit squads armed with M60 light machine guns and RPGs, the MSGs receive extensive training in the fundamentals of guerrilla warfare and special operations. All MSGs are volunteers and are considered the finest soldier in the battalion. "They are man for man," according to Commandant D., "the best soldiers in all of Ireland."

Every bomb call in Dundalk is handled as a major military undertaking—especially after Omagh. The town of Omagh, County Tyrone, in Northern Ireland, had hoped that Saturday August 16, 1998 would be a peaceful summer day without any security incidents. Hundreds of people, in town for a carnival walked through picturesque streets enjoying a bright sunny day in a land praying for peace. At 2:30 in the afternoon, in typical terrorist fashion, a call came into the offices of a Belfast television station warning of a bomb set to go off in Omagh on high street. Forty minutes later, as police were evacuating the area, the 500 lb. car bomb exploded several hundred yards away at the junction of market street and Dublin road, where people had gathered thinking they

* Identity withheld for security considerations.

* Identity withheld for security considerations.

*The Hobo once again swings into action.*

*The Hobo robot in action—what was once a briefcase in a car park is soon shattered by the explosive force of a disrupter's round.*

*An Alouette III from the Irish Army Air Wing prepares to take off from the parade ground at the Dundalk military camp to hover over an EOD call out near the border.*

*With an intelligence officer in tow, an Alouette III from the Irish Army Air Wing prepares to support an EOD call out near the border. Helicopters are the primary mode of tactical support for Irish units serving along the Bandit Country border with Ireland.*

were out of harm's way. The carnage in Omagh, the worst terrorist bombing in the tragic history of the Northern Ireland troubles, was horrific. Thirty had died in the blast, over 200 had been seriously wounded. It was but one of a long line of deadly bombing attacks that have shattered thousands of lives and dotted the scenic countryside of the Irish isles in pools of blood. The Omagh bombing killed thirty men, women and children. Catholics and Protestants were killed, side-by-side, in the blast. The car bomb, carried out by a splinter group of the Provisional IRA opposed to the peace accords, was state-of-the art bomb-making that bomb-technicians on both sides of the border have had to come up close and personal with on numerous occasions. When Irish police arrested several suspects for their roles in producing the deadly bomb that killed and maimed so many at Omagh, five hailed from Dundalk.

Irish Army EOD officers know that much of material and expertise behind bombing attacks like the Omagh carnage originate in their own backyard. Many terrorist bombs that find their way up north originate in the south, where a cottage industry of bomb-component building production lines produce state-of-the art devices destined for the northern six counties. Handling them before they reach their destination is the job of the Irish defense forces bomb officers and the MSGs in Dundalk.

On one call on a gray and gloomy March morning at the Dundalk barracks, the noise of choppers engulfs in the air (British Lynx transports to the north and Irish Alouette IIIs in the south). Sitting inside the officer's mess, drinking a cup of tea and catching up on the football scores, the on-call EOD officer, Commandant S., receives word of a device along the border on his secure pager. Tossing his tea on the bar, he calls the operation sergeant and races toward the EOD barracks where he must assemble a crew and take his robot and equipment toward the device. The MSGs receive word of the incident at the same time, and leave their recreation room to suit up, grab their load bearing devices and their Steyr assault rifles, and fire up the engines in their fleet of Toyota 4x4s. Commandant S. and the MSG commander confer, check coordinates on a highly-detailed map, and hold their breath—the device is supposed to be a haphazard contraption built on a beer barrel. Such a device can hold some twenty-kilos of explosives and enough shrapnel to kill a company of infantrymen. The drive to the border takes all of three minutes.

The border between north and south is an amalgam of jagged and descending slopes, plush green fields, and all too often, invisible and disputed frontier markers. It is a no man's land and a ground zero wrapped neatly into one lethal war zone for men, on both sides of the fence, tasked with handling explosive devices. Terrorists hoping to hit a British patrol or a Royal Ulster Constabulary vehicle will often set their device on the British side of the frontier, and operate the device, courtesy of control wires, safely in the south. For the bomb techs there is no room for error in bandit country. For the bomb tech, the less sophisticated devices, like those

*Awaiting the arrival of the EOD truck, the MSG's scan the frontier for any signs of terrorist activity.*

*With their Steyrs at the ready, the MSGs greet the arrival of the Garda liaison officer and the EOD truck at a suspect device at the border. The 27th Infantry's coat of arms—with service in Lebanon and along the border with Bandit Country in Dundalk, it is one of the elite infantry formations in the Irish Defense Forces.*

During a call out for a device situated "directly" on the border, operators from the 27th Infantry Mobile Security Group prepare an operational plan.

MSGs mill about in front of the EOD truck, as the bomb tech officer confers with his counterpart in the Garda.

Close-up view of the newly-issued "speckled" camouflage fatigues issued to Irish special forces.

With his Steyr 5.56mm assault rifle at the ready, a 27th Infantry MSG NCO moves into position.

*With the Mobile Security Group in a defensive perimeter, Commandant S. readies his Hobo for action.*

used by the Protestant paramilitaries, are more volatile to deal with. The Protestant paramilitaries, who have operated on both sides of the border, are known for their simple bomb designs that are sometimes most dangerous to render safe. While Irish bomb techs are called to a diverse array of incidents, from Michael Collins military campaign against the British in 1916 to World War Two sea mines that wash across the Irish shore, the unit's primary work revolves around terrorist bombs. The Provisional IRA in particular is legendary for their ingenious skill in designing and producing, sometimes on a large-scale, highly sophisticated explosive devices and delivery systems.

Once Commandant S. and the MSGs reach the scene, the dozen heavily armed infantrymen deploy to a perimeter marked by weapons at the ready. Several MSGs reah to the very boundaries of the frontier, kneel to one knee, and peer through the sights of the Steyr assault rifle. Fingers caress triggers as the soldiers search the surrounding hills and trees for any signs of IRA activity. The team leader will check with each of his men along the widened circular perimeter to see if the area is hot or cold. Hot areas of operation, where terrorist activity is confirmed, will warrant over-flights of choppers by both the Irish Army's air wing and, through liaison

*Wearing his characteristic beret in the field, a 27th Infantry MSG assumes a firing position, in search of terrorists just fifty meters to the north across the frontier. From Lebanon to the Irish frontier, the Irish Defense Forces have served in some of the world's most hotly contested guerrilla battlefields.*

*An MSG takes aim with his Steyr assault rifle—tasked with eliminating any possible threat to the EOD crew with terminating firepower. With its sturdy and light construction, the Irish Defense Forces—and its special forces in the field—have found the Steyr to be a weapon ideally suited to the rugged Irish landscape.*

*With his weapon aimed directly across the border, a 27th Infantry MSG stands at the ready to protect Commandant S. and his crew of EOD officers. According to IRA and Protestant paramilitary operatives captured along the border, the terrorists have great respect for the determination and skill of the Irish MSGs.*

Commandant S. (right) prepares the charge on the Hobo's disrupter prior to tackling the suspect device on the border.

Just yards from the Northern Irish border, Commandant S.'s Hobo explodes into action.

Until the last bits of explosives and gear are back on the EOD truck, the MSGs continue to cover and protect the bomb crew's activities.

communication links, with British troops across the border. Cold areas of operation are where the perimeter around the suspect device is considered safe. On this dark and gloomy morning, the perimeter is cold. Commandant S. can go to work.

The robot has become the safest tactic for bomb techs all over the world, from Israel to New York City, to render devices safe through remote means. The Irish-designed and built Hobo robot, a highly-maneuverable wheeled device considered the best such device in the world, is a mainstay of the Irish Defense Forces EOD teams and ideally suited for the wet and muddy ground found around Dundalk. Having suited up in a Canadian-built cocoon of Kevlar, Commandant S. guides the Hobo until it is directly in front of the suspect barrel. Commandant S. guides his robot toward the suspected device using a joystick and a mounted camera. As he guides the robot through the muddy track, he lowers the robot's arm and the mounted disrupter so that it is aimed pointblank over where the experienced bomb tech believes a detonator might be positioned, can destroy the device's operational mechanism before it can explode. As the MSGs move into a wider perimeter, Commandant S. flips a switch that fires his robot's disrupter. The barrel evaporates into a cloud of white smoke and shrapnel. An abandoned beer keg that caused such concern is suddenly reduced to a shattered and distorted sliver of battered metal.

With the robot's work done, Commandant S. must make a manual determination that the suspected device has been successfully rendered safe. Suiting up in a hulking green Kevlar suit of armor, Commandant S. grabs a pole and walks the fifty yards to the smoldering remnants of the keg. This is the time that the MSGs are most concerned. In order to send a daunting message to other EOD officer, an IRA or Protestant paramilitary sniper armed with an Armalite could let off a round aimed at the bomb tech's Plexiglas visor, the most vulnerable piece of protective clothing worn by the bomb officer. "Anything in the treeline?," one of the MSGs utters over his field radio to an Alouette flying overhead, "let us know if you see any Tango activity."

After examining the beer keg, Commandant S. kneels cumbersomely in his heavy suit to see if there was any explosives or detonators inside the metal drum. Offering a thumb's up, he indicates to all that the situation is safe. Nearly two hours after the first call of the device, Commandant S. removes his heavy Kevlar body armor and loads his robot and explosive charges back onto the truck. The MSGs remain on guard, though, as terrorists in Ireland have been known to steal explosives any way they can—even hijacking military convoys.

Ireland's primary hope for a peaceful future depends on the ability of the security forces on both sides of the border to neutralize the destructive wishes of the radicals while the politicians and the men and women who will be forced to co-exist on one island. For the Irish army bomb techs and their protective cover of MSGs, they know all too well that they will be challenged in the months to come—to not only prevent catastrophes like Omagh, but to ensure that their embattled country will progress toward a peaceful future.